Accidental Lives

First published in 2024

By Black Spring Press
An imprint of Eyewear Publishing Limited
The Black Spring Press Group

Cover design by Matt Broughton
Interior typeset by Edwin Smet
Authors' photograph on the backcover by David Myers
Cover image credited to Alan Harper/*Financial Times* © Financial Times Limited. Printed with kind permission. All rights reserved.

All rights reserved
© 2024 Sylvia Holder and Lindsay Swan

The moral right of the authors has been asserted.

All rights reserved
Without limiting the rights under copyright reserved above, no part of this publication may be reproduced, stored in or introduced into a retrieval system, or transmitted, in any form or by any means (electronic, mechanical, photocopying, recording or otherwise), without the prior written permission of both the copyright owners and the above publisher of this book.

Set in Bembo 12 / 14,5 pt
ISBN 978-1-915406-86-6

WWW.BLACKSPRINGPRESSGROUP.COM

Accidental Lives

How two intrepid women travelled the world, ran an unconventional PR company and set up a charity in India

Sylvia Holder & Lindsay Swan

To

JR, Ali and Aarthi

CONTENTS

PART THREE

PROLOGUE

'WHAT'S YOUR NAME AND WHERE YOU COME FROM?'

by Sylvia

'What's your name and where you come from?'

The uncertain, quick-fire English seemed to come from nowhere. I looked down to see a little boy dressed in a faded red T-shirt and blue shorts, as skinny as they come but with a smile that lit up his face and captured my immediate attention.

'Hello there,' I replied. 'My name is Sylvia and I come from London.' I returned the smile as he scrunched up his nose, trying the three syllables of my name out for size.

It was 1989, and we were standing on the beach of Kovalam, a fishing village near Chennai in South India. I was on a business trip and had walked there from my posh Taj hotel, which was situated incongruously on the edge of the village, its manicured beach a fitting demarcation between the haves and the have-nots. When I passed through Kovalam on my way to my client's office in Chennai, the extreme poverty there was painfully evident.

Luxury can pall, particularly when you become aware of a poor village just a few yards from the indulgences of the hotel. From the beach, I could see the fishermen's boats and decided to wander along in the hope of having a chat with some of them, their English permitting. How nice to stroll along the Coromandel Coast, I thought, the waves gently lapping on the golden sands, the palm trees waving in the gentle breeze … Wrong! Once away from the swept white sands of the hotel, the beach was strewn with household rubbish and even human excrement. Shoes were a must. This was not the place to feel the sand trickling through your toes.

I was in luck. A few fishermen were mending their nets in readiness for their overnight fishing expedition, but before I had a chance to speak to them, the little boy seized my attention. I soon discovered that he was Venkatraman, known as Venkat, twelve years old and a fisherman's son, the youngest of six siblings. He took me over to his father's fishing boat. It had seen better days, the ravages of the sea testament to its age. Luckily, it was still serviceable as without it there would be no fish, thus no income.

'My father fishes every night and doesn't get back until the sun comes up,' Venkat told me. 'If he catches a lot, we can have fish for supper but usually he needs to sell them all. Then we just eat rice and vegetables.'

'Where does he sell the fish?' I asked.

'The big fish are sold to the hotels and restaurants in Chennai, the smaller ones in the fish market in the village.' His waif-like appearance was confirmation of the daily struggle his father faced just to keep his family fed. 'I show you my village?' he suggested.

There wasn't much hesitation on my part. 'Yes, please.'

I'd seen the road leading out of Kovalam, but this was an opportunity to walk around an off-the-beaten-track Indian village with a resident. For Venkat, this was a chance to earn himself a few much-needed rupees. Off we went, Venkat carefully guiding his guest through the warren of alleys between the tumbledown houses. Some of them had concrete walls with a palm leaf roof; others were made entirely of leaves and were flimsy at best. Holes were often covered up with an equally holey tarpaulin in an attempt to keep the contents dry. We walked past women drawing water from the well, children playing, dogs, goats, cows and chickens feeding off scraps. All life was here. I saw a woman washing the family's clothes in the street with a bucket of water, a bar of soap and a big stone, grabbing each piece of clothing at one end and slamming the rest of it onto the stone to remove the dirt. Meanwhile, other women cooked their families' meagre meals on an open wood fire outside their homes. Rubbish was strewn everywhere and the houses themselves were shabby and ill-kempt. Venkat showed me the inside of a couple of them. I had to bend low to squeeze through the door into a stuffy, airless space with no windows or furniture. Just a couple of roll-up mats on the ground to sleep on.

The obvious poverty was distressing.

I heard more about Venkat and his family on our walkabout. Although poor, he was a happy little boy from a loving family.

'We laugh a lot,' he told me, which cheered me, considering their circumstances. The eight of them lived in a small ramshackle two-roomed house. 'We all sleep in the main room on the floor, but as it's so crowded, my brother Janaki and I often sleep on the beach and we make our pillows of sand. We're the two youngest in the family,' he added, by way of explanation.

'Don't your parents worry about you on the beach?' I asked.

'We're only a few yards away, and it means there's

more sleeping room in the house for the others.'

There was no running water or sanitary arrangements: a shower consisted of a bucket of water drawn from the well poured over their heads, while personal matters were basic in the extreme. No public facilities were available so open land or the beach were the only options. Flies were abundant, and the stench in some places hard to stomach.

Venkat must have needed a good meal, as I found myself being steered into a scruffy café where mysteriously two of his pals had materialised. I bought fish and prawns for the four of us, and tucked into the best prawns I'd ever tasted, straight from the sea. They all eagerly accepted doggy bags, and heaps of prawns and fish were wrapped up in banana leaves to take home to their families. From his companions, I managed to glean more about my guide. Venkat was obviously popular and kind, but he was no angel and got himself into a fair few scrapes. He loved football and was a talented player, unlike most of his contemporaries, who lived for the national game of cricket.

The tour and sustenance stop-off over, Venkat took me back to the beach so I could walk back to my posh hotel.

When it came time to part ways, he got straight to the point. 'Can you give me £10 for my school fees, please?'

I pondered his request. 'Don't you get free education?'

I wondered if the request was a ruse – not that I minded, as I had that amount in mind as a parting gift anyway, having greatly enjoyed my time spent with this delightful boy. But his reply in faltering English was worrying.

'There's no free education after the age of twelve and my father cannot afford the fees for a private school.'

He explained that 8,000 people lived in the village,

which was more like a small town, but free education for all the children hit the buffers after primary school. No wonder life on the breadline was rampant with no escape.

'I'll give you the £10,' I said and added, on the spur of the moment, 'and I'll also pay for the rest of your education. And, if you can make it, your fees for university.'

The whole idea was ludicrous. His father would surely want him to leave school to help him mend the fishing nets and bring in the catch, and the idea of a boy from such a poor family going to university was absurd. Yet, what can I say? My impulsiveness has ruled my life.

Initially, Venkat said nothing but looked thoughtful. Then he beamed from ear to ear as he tucked the rupees into the pocket of his shorts.

I found a scrap of paper on which I wrote my address. 'Let me know if you'd like to take up my offer,' I said, as I took my leave, returning to a world apart from where I'd just spent one of the best afternoons of my life.

PART ONE

CHAPTER 1
CHILDHOOD

by Sylvia

The story goes that my pregnant mother Jean sat in a hot bath and drank gin to get rid of me, as her doctor had advised her that any more children would pose a serious health risk. Before me, my mama had given birth to three children in eleven-and-a-half months: John, born in 1934, then twins Robert (Bob) and Richard, but sadly Richard survived only ten days. She was seriously ill after their birth and any more pregnancies would be ill-advised. I suspect the gin solution was weak as, despite the health warnings, she desperately wanted another baby, with fingers firmly crossed that it would be a girl. I duly made my appearance in the world on 6 December 1938.

I was born in Lytham St Anne's, near Blackpool, but can remember little of my early years there. We moved back to my parents' home town, the north London suburb of Finchley, in 1944 during the dying months of the war. I have a vague recollection of the doodlebugs and sirens, and the family's gas masks hanging in the hall. I had a Mickey Mouse mask but it bore little resemblance to the mouse apart from its bright red and blue colours.

The empty house next door had been bombed before our arrival and was boarded up, but those who did the boarding hadn't reckoned on the ingenuity of my brothers, and it soon became our playground. Toys and dolls were scattered around the remains of the building which I was delighted about, not understanding the grim significance.

The war finally ended, and on VJ Day the family went to Bournemouth for a holiday. My mother kept a scrappy little drawing I did on the train of marching soldiers and flags complete with the inscription, *The war is over and it is Wansday*. It's now in a remarkable five-inch-thick scrapbook-cum-diary, which she wrote in longhand and kept up until the age of ninety-one.

I had a happy childhood, if poor – but that's to be expected if you're a preacher's kid. As the country was all on stringent food rationing during and after the war, it made little difference if you were rich or poor. I was fifteen years old by the time all rationing came to an end. It seems difficult to believe these days but, for example, we were each allowed just one fresh egg every week, two ounces of butter (and four ounces of margarine) and three ounces of sweets.

My parents were warm people and they loved their children unconditionally. They weren't demonstrative when compared to today's 'love you' mantra, but we knew, come what may, they were there for us. Perhaps that's why I've never had any hang-ups about my childhood or the need for a psychiatrist's couch. Love, stability and laughter and perhaps a teeny bit of jealousy of my wealthier friends are how I remember my young days. Lots of hand-me-down clothes and books and toys came from church members, which we accepted as normal. We were, however, the envy of many of our better-off friends as our house always had the latest train sets and the biggest Meccano boxes, thanks to my parents' friendship with Roland and Maudie Hornby.

Hornby is still recognised as the maker of the best state-of-the-art electric train sets.

My father, Jack, was tall and impressive looking, universally loved and highly regarded, both in the pulpit and out. His faith had a profound influence on people, through both his outstanding preaching and his pastoral work, but he never tried to indoctrinate his children. He was broad-minded and receptive to other people's ideas and philosophies. His Christian example had a quiet but positive influence on me, and although I became a non-believer in my adult years, I hope I've inherited the principles by which he lived. He was quite theatrical in the pulpit but not in the hell, fire and brimstone sense: instead he drew on his love of the arts for inspiration, peppering his sermons with humour and theatrical touches. If he referred to Marks, it could be St Mark's Gospel, Karl Marx, Marks & Spencer or the Marx Brothers. Regardless, he got his message over and the congregation loved him.

He was wily, too. One day a speed cop stopped him when he was exceeding the limit.

My father looked heavenwards. 'I'm so sorry, Officer, but you must understand that my mind was on higher things and I simply hadn't realised the speed I was going.'

Needless to say, he escaped a speeding ticket.

Another trick of his was to wear his dog collar on train journeys, ensuring he had the carriage to himself.

When not working, you would find him at the library or with his nose in a book at home. He was a John Galsworthy fan and loved *The Forsyte Saga* serial on television, as most of Britain did. It was shown on a Sunday evening and it clashed with the end of the evening service. Not in my father's church it didn't: curiously for twenty-six weeks the sermon was shorter than usual and when announcing the last hymn, he would say 'Hymn number 210, omitting verses two, five and six.' And home he sped!

There was a large Sunday School, not least because the children came to the church for the early part of the service, which included a children's story with a moral message. The kids adored my father and were rapt with his off-the-cuff stories. Not for his own children did bunny rabbits and kittens feature. He terrified us – which, of course, we loved – with gruesome stories of the antics of the diabolical bloodhound of supernatural origin that haunted Dartmoor, freely ad-libbed from Conan Doyle's *The Hound of the Baskervilles.* 'It was a dark and stormy night...' was the inevitable opening line to his tales of the terrifying dog and his night-time marauding.

My pa was never happier than when he was with his children, not only when we were young, but to the end of his days, when we were in our fifties and sixties. He never tired of hearing about our lives and was always there for some quiet words of wisdom – as was my mother – when any of our lives were running off track.

My mother was a sensitive person. When Richard died aged just ten days, she wrote about her sadness in her journal but, as she still had Bob and toddler John, showed more concern for the mother of the baby who shared Richard's incubator and also died. She would be going home without any baby.

While supportive of my father, my ma had a life outside the ministry. She was a fearless go-getter and discovered a flair for buying and selling houses, which proved a nice little earner to supplement my father's stipend. I inherited her love of wheeling and dealing in bricks and mortar. She bought her first buy-to-let house, a large Victorian building in Bexhill, for £2,000 in 1954 and converted it into four flats. Today's value for the four of them is in the region of £560,000!

She bought, converted, let and sold until her final buy in 1963, her *pièce de résistance*, Avon Castle, set in four acres of beautiful Hampshire countryside and flanked by a 230-yard stretch of the River Avon with salmon-fishing rights. It had already been converted into nine flats and my parents lived in the imposing, if not totally practical, ground floor flat that swept around the building. The castle was built for the Earl of Egmont in 1875 for £80,000, the equivalent of £224,000 in 1961, but my mother bought it for the astonishing price of £16,500 at what must have been a poorly attended auction. Buying castles did not sit easily with her church role and would doubtless be considered inappropriate by the church members. In deference to my father, and his possible embarrassment at such a revelation, she declined to give her name at the auction and became 'The mystery woman in the red hat' in the publicity about her purchase. It backfired horribly, as she was soon identified and the local press had a field day.

My ma borrowed every penny from the bank (as was easy to do in the early sixties), which she was able to repay speedily from the sale of the other flats. What a coup! I don't think I ever gave her the credit she deserved for her business acumen. Eccentric she was, but there were no flies on my mama. The castle was sold on long ago, but the family still has associations with it as my nephew James bought a flat there several years ago for weekend visits. There have been many happy family picnics alongside the beautiful stretch of river.

My maternal grandparents were quite austere and formal, and my grandfather always wore a wing collar. He was a ship broker and worked at the impressive Baltic Exchange in the City.[1] They lived in a sizeable Edwardian house in Finchley and visiting them was always an ordeal. My brothers and I often had to suppress our giggles when we were with Granny.

'When are you going back to school, dear?' she would ask. Then, five minutes later, 'When are you going back to school, dear?' and so it went on, the same question over and over again. I don't think she had dementia but she certainly had serious loss of memory.

I never knew my paternal grandparents. By all accounts my grandfather had a colourful life, making and losing big sums of money regularly. My grandmother might be ordering her food shopping from Harrods one week and queuing at the soup kitchen the next. I gathered he had a glad eye for the girls too. My father was actually at his father's funeral as I was being born and my grandmother had died a few months before.

My paternal great-grandfather had many a claim to fame. I discovered a lot about him from an Ilford newspaper cutting in August 1909 – that he was not only kissed by the soon-to-be Queen Victoria when he was a baby, but many years later saved her life. His mother was taking him in his pram for an airing in Uckfield Park when the Earl of Liverpool, who was chaperoning Princess Victoria, walked by. As the Earl knew the baby's mother (my great-great-grandmother), he stopped to speak to her, and the young Queen-in-waiting asked if she could kiss the baby.

1 This building was destroyed by an IRA bomb in 1992 and The Gherkin now stands on the site.

Seventeen years later on 27 June 1850, he joined a crowd to see the Queen pass along Piccadilly in her open landau when an assailant, Robert Pate, aimed a violent blow on her head with a heavy gold-headed cane. Great-grandfather to the rescue: he rushed forward, diverted the blow, got a fair whack of it himself but saved the Queen, except for the royal bonnet, which was knocked off her head. The police seized her saviour, thinking he was the assailant until witnesses assured them he was the hero.

Great-grandfather was a man of many parts who led a colourful life with a varied career, not least fathering eleven children, my grandfather being the seventh. Apart from saving the life of the sovereign, he was the Special Messenger to the United States Legation in London, the Chief Examiner of Coins at the Royal Mint and, in the latter part of his life, was ordained as a Congregational minister. One of his duties as the Messenger to the US Legation was to meet the despatch bag from the American Government on its arrival at Euston Station, and, never letting it out of his possession, take it to the Legation in Piccadilly. On one occasion his taxi was stopped close to his destination to make way for the Duke of Wellington, the Iron Duke. Great-grandfather jumped out of the taxi and was collared by several policemen, but he extricated himself as nothing was going to stop him delivering his precious package. The duke's delay by this impudent young man caused much consternation but when the reason was explained to the duke, he summoned the boy.

'Young man,' he addressed him, 'you are just beginning life. I am closing mine, but I congratulate you on your conduct tonight. You overcame all obstacles to do your duty. Go on as you have begun, and success will crown your efforts.' He shook his hand and gave him a sovereign.

***

I got on well with my brothers, although we were all different. Bob was always up to mischief and generally got away with murder but not on one memorable occasion. He and John had fixed four old pram wheels onto a wooden crate into which Bob deposited me and pushed me along the road. Unfortunately, the road went downhill and he couldn't hold on as the crate gathered speed. Off I careered over a busy crossroads with my mother, screaming like a banshee, in hot pursuit. While I managed to escape unscathed, the perpetrator of the crime had to face a very angry mother, although I doubt the punishment was too severe.

My father's stipend was also bolstered by three generations of our Siamese cats: Sally, Alex and Fleur. We all adored them and they earned their keep by producing pedigree progeny for which we got the princely sum of seven guineas each (unless Bob had let out a cat on heat, resulting in varying shades of kittens. This happened more than once). It instilled in me a lifelong love of cats and, over the years, I have had a couple of Burmese, a Siamese and an Abyssinian and, so far, six elderly rescue cats. I love them all so much that I wonder when they die why I have them, such is the grief.

Our holiday one year was in Southampton where we had a house swap with friends. The eccentric parents decided they would make the ninety-mile journey from Finchley in north London to the south coast on their new mopeds, which were nothing more than bicycles with small motors. Extraordinarily, twelve-year-old John was put in charge of his younger siblings, the cats and the luggage on the train journey to Southampton. Even at that age he was responsible and reliable – and still is. The moped riders survived their journey, but surprise, surprise, we had our parents with us on the way home, the bikes stowed in the guard's van.

I used to cycle to our primary school with my friend and neighbour, Meg, which astounds me now as we were only seven or eight. How lucky we were that we didn't have to be driven to and from school. How different things were then. Meg became a lifelong friend and I'm a proud godmother of her son Nick. I don't remember much about the school, other than being severely reprimanded by the headmistress for hitting a girl with a ruler, according to the 'victim'. I would happily have hit the silly girl many times but I was innocent of the crime and wasn't going to take the rap for something I didn't do. For me, it became a bit of a *Winslow Boy* case as, even at that young age, I was incensed at being accused of doing something I hadn't done. It upset me so much that my father was obliged to take up the cudgel on my behalf to set the headmistress right. My concern for injustice has remained with me all my life.

I went to boarding school when I was nine. Rather than being dragged there screaming, I actively wanted to go, doubtless influenced by Enid Blyton's *Malory Towers* and with John and Bob already away at school. We all went to schools where children of the cloth were heavily subsidised. Milton Mount College was in Sussex in a beautiful but crumbling Victorian mansion which used to belong to the Montefiores, an eminent family of diplomats and bankers. Half the classrooms were subterranean. The central heating pipes were lukewarm. We weren't allowed to sit on them as we'd get piles. No carpets, no curtains, lots of buckets collecting leaking water. Spinster teachers, some unqualified. The food was horrible and there wasn't enough of it, but this was only three years after the war ended, after all. On a positive note, we did have good sporting facilities including a swimming pool, but the downside was mandatory swimming even at the beginning of a freezing cold summer term. If we couldn't play games because of the weather, we were chucked out anyway in snow, blizzard, storm or tempest for an hour's walk in a crocodile.

The only time we were allowed home during term-time during the eight-year incarceration was for Queen Elizabeth's Coronation in June 1953. While millions watched it on a tiny flickering black-and-white television – which we didn't have – my parents decided that we should all be there in person to witness such an important historical occasion. I remember it vividly, not least because of the pouring rain, but we had a good view of the Queen and all the other carriages from our stance on Cockspur Street, which seemed less crowded than the rest of the five-mile route. Another queen who stole the limelight that day was Queen Salote of Tonga, 6' 3" tall, almost as broad and with a smile to match, she captivated the spectators as she rode in her open carriage in the teeming rain, refusing to close the top.

The Dickensian lifestyle at the school was illustrated by my punishment for talking after lights out. For such a heinous crime I was condemned to solitary confinement for three days. I slept in a room on my own, ate solo at a table, sat apart from my classmates during lessons. I was forbidden to speak to anyone. A leper. I was just ten years old.

Strangely, I think that barbaric treatment at such a

young age for such a minor offence coloured the rest of my schooldays. It didn't scare me, far from it, but I took on board then that I needed to look out for myself and not comply with how 'they' wanted to shape me. Treat me as you will, but I will not bend to the mould you'd like me to fill. I became a fiercely independent rebel. I was happy, had lots of friends and can't remember ever being homesick.

Sometime later, a group of us were caught climbing a tree and our punishment, meted out by the headmistress, was to weed the Dutch Garden where only the staff were allowed. We enjoyed it so much that when my turn to sit next to the HM at lunch on the top table came round, I had the temerity to say, 'Miss Farrell, we wondered if you would like us to continue with the weeding of the Dutch garden, we much enjoyed doing it.'

Unusually for her, she was nonplussed that we should have *enjoyed* our punishment. 'I think not,' came the reply.

The tree is still there, and I've seen it recently. The school itself closed down a few years after my departure to give way for an enormous sixties-style and quite hideous concrete block of 146 flats. Its saving grace was the preservation of the school's wonderful grounds, which are open to the public and still remain much as they were in my day: a big round pond with water lilies and a fountain, a camellia walk, masses of rhododendron bushes and, yes, a Dutch Garden. When in the area, I sometimes take a stroll down memory lane.

I liked my rebel status, although 'youth is wasted on the young' was apt in my case as I didn't take advantage of the learning opportunities, such as they were. I preferred to play to the gallery, a comment which appeared more than once in the headmistress's end of term report. Midnight feasts, courtesy of the kitchen, were more my and my cohorts' scene: the hidden keys were easily found and we were noticeably fatter than our law-abiding friends. Late evening, after lights out, sometimes saw us escaping Colditz, walking the mile to Three Bridges station and taking a train to Crawley. The chippy was still open in the then small town, and after a wander around we took the train back and were soon back in our beds. Batty Hatty, my best friend at school and one of the few school friends still on this mortal coil, recently reminded me that on one occasion we'd been spotted by a mistress while devouring our chips on the streets of Crawley. We'd blown it. We were nervous the next day waiting for the inevitable call to the headmistress's room. It wouldn't be weeding the Dutch Garden this time. Might we be expelled? Panic. But the call never came.

All the teachers lived in, a bedroom being their only private space, the BBC Home Service their only company. It must have been a sad life for them. I hope they had a stash of sherry hidden away. The only pair of trousers in the place belonged to George the maintenance man.

There was an anomaly to my rebellious persona: I was a Girl Guide. This was to please my mother, whose guiding days in one form or another stayed with her throughout her life. She loved all the jolly hockey sticks antics and I still have all her guiding paraphernalia. It includes an array of proficiency badges. For her skills as a cook she had to know how to wash up, wait at table, and skin and clean a rabbit, while for her needlewoman badge she had to make her own skirt and, of all things, knickers!

I might have been a Queen's Guide had I not failed the last of the tests before the grand finale. It was needlework that let me down but mercifully not knicker-making. The

Guide captain, music mistress Miss Lee, nicknamed Lobster because of her flushed cheeks, surprised me by failing my perfectly acceptable effort. I could sew and still can. I sussed why I had failed – Lobster's pet, Rosie, had failed the grand finale and she didn't want me to upstage her, given that I probably had more initiative and oomph than Rosie had. I hope Lobster had a conscience about it. In retrospect, I'm surprised I didn't challenge her and demand a second opinion. Not that I would have got one, but I would have made my point. I was upset.

I served an eight-year sentence at Milton Mount and, not surprisingly, emerged with just four O-levels, which weren't going to trail a glittering academic career for me. It should have been four and a half, as I passed my French oral but failed the written exam. I had the clever wheeze of putting my padded arm in a sling as it was a dead cert that the questions would be about my 'injury', and I duly mugged up on my subject. The examiner fell for it. Her inevitable opening question, '*Qu'as-tu fait à ton bras?*' got my quick-fire answer in *parfait Français: 'Je suis tombée dans les escaliers et je me suis cassée le bras.'*

My fluency flagged somewhat after more chat about my unfortunate arm, but it was good enough to get me a pass. Shame about the written exam.

Throughout my incarceration, my hideous green tunic – with permanent box pleats to hide any suspicion of a bosom – was devoid of any badges of merit: form captain, good deportment, lacrosse captain, head girl. In fact, I was the only one in the Lower VI who *wasn't* a prefect. I should have worn its non-existence as a badge of honour but I think I was miffed to be so obviously excluded. But I had my days in the sun many years later when in 2012 I won *The Times*

Sternberg Active Life Award, which is awarded to people over seventy who have made an 'outstanding contribution to the community and to public life', and in the 2019 New Year's Honours I received a British Empire Medal (BEM) 'for services to education in Kovalam, India'.

Bah humbug to a prefect's badge.

We had no career guidance as such but one of the teachers took it upon herself to give us career ideas. Presenting me with just two options – shorthand/typing or marriage – she looked me up and down and shook her head sadly at my nuptial prospects.

'I don't think we can expect any early marriage proposals, but shorthand and typing should suit your capabilities well,' she said, not unkindly.

So shorthand and typing it was. 'Dimwits this way please.' What a huge favour she did me: those mundane skills took me around the world.

The strange thing is that I was happy at school and look back on my schooldays with affection. They gave me independence and confidence, for which I'm grateful.

My 'finishing school' was the council's College of Commerce in Bristol, my family home at the time, where a year's secretarial course cost a princely five quid. I was an ace – and still am – at touch typing, but the squiggle language of shorthand was something else. I had no problems getting it down reasonably accurately and speedily, but drew a blank when it came to reading it back. A dyslexia of squiggles.

Thus an equally pessimistic college tutor presented me with a limited choice: 'We shouldn't have a problem finding you a position where shorthand won't be needed. Insurance companies use dictating machines, so a job in the typing pool of an insurance company should suit you well.'

Obviously, a thrilling life lay ahead of me.

'I'd prefer to work for a newspaper or the local BBC. Maybe I should approach them?' I mooted.

More sad and incredulous shakes of the head at such an impossible suggestion.

One thing was for sure in my mind. I would not be joining an insurance company to type my life away.

I wrote to three local newspapers, the BBC and other interesting-sounding companies that might give me a foothold in a future career. And luck was on my side. I was summoned for an interview at the *Bristol Evening World* and on 2 September 1957 I walked through their impressive portals to begin my first job as Private and Confidential Secretary, no less, to the General Manager and the Editor.

CHAPTER 2
WORKING GIRL

by Sylvia

Working at the *Evening World* was great fun. As a raw rookie, the early days were nerve-wracking but I soon settled down. Both the General Manager, Alan Bonner, and the Editor, Dai Morgan, were affable, the GM keener on the golf course than his office. Many the time I had to ring the golf club with a message for him that the Managing Director of the Group was on his way to see him. The very Welsh Dai Morgan, always with pipe in mouth like so many men of his time, was pleasant enough if somewhat uncommunicative. He certainly didn't fit the typical image of an editor shouting at his terrified subordinates. I once had the temerity to correct his grammar. He had handwritten a letter for typing and I changed his 'Thank you for inviting my wife and I' to a 'me'. He insisted on the incorrect version.

I loved working with the journalists, among whom were the prolific playwright-to-be, Tom Stoppard, and future *Times* editor, Charlie Wilson. It was good socially too, with lots of pub visits and plenty of boyfriend material. Sunday afternoon tennis matches together with the other papers – the Bristol *Evening Post* and the *Western Daily Press* – were also highlights.

The newsroom was redolent of its era, full of cigarette smoke and clanking ancient typewriters. The chief reporter and his hip flask of whisky were never separated and I don't think I ever saw him sober. I got in with a bit of journalism too – I took over the children's page, though heaven knows what I wrote about, kids' subjects not being my forte.

During the printing strike of 1959, I became a linotype operator. A blackleg. This was the worst printing strike for more than thirty years and revolved around the printing ink section of the industry, most of whom were on strike. Initially, only the provincial newspapers were affected but it spread to the nationals when their ink dried up. A bitter dispute, it lasted six weeks. In this time, I became a proficient hot metal typesetter and, together with some journalists, management and anyone around from the three Bristol newspapers, we proudly produced one edition a day. I thoroughly enjoyed the experience and I'm sure I never gave it another thought as to whether the strike was justified, and my archive reading has made me none the wiser.

The *Evening World* always had excellent journalists, many of whom went on to Fleet Street, but the better circulation *Evening Post* was visually more appealing. It doubtless had a more up-to-date printing press.

After a couple of years, I decided it was time to move on. I still loved the job but was ready to leave the provinces and seek my fortune, or at least some fun, in the Big Smoke. That was in 1959, and sadly the *Evening World* was to survive for only another three years. I wonder if the printing strike hastened the demise.

My Vespa and I bid a fond farewell to Bristol and we arrived in London, where I rented a flat with three girlfriends: Sally, a schoolfriend; Frances, who had been a copytaker on the paper; and Jill, another Bristolian. What a different London it was in the late fifties from today's modern metropolis. Our expectations were low, which was just as well as our abode was a freezing cold, shabby flat. However, it was situated in Queen's Gate, South Kensington, which was a brilliant place to be – close to the West End and with lots going on in South Ken itself, not least the V&A, Natural History and Science Museums, and numerous good pubs and restaurants. We shared bedrooms and the bathroom was shared by yet two more girls in another flat. An ancient and temperamental Ascot water heater occasionally spat out some tepid water.

The bathing situation was unwittingly solved by the Regent Palace Hotel in Piccadilly Circus. It was respectable in those days but it sank into seediness and finally closed in 2006. I'd stayed at the hotel with my mother and recalled that there were bathrooms dotted around the bedroom floors, ensuite bathrooms being unusual then. There was no security in 1960, so along I would trot with my sponge bag, take a lift to my chosen floor and enjoy soaking in an enormous bath with endless hot water and big fluffy towels. On departure I rang the bell for maid service. QED.

Clean I might be, but I needed some sustenance too. What better place than the Hilton Hotel and Grosvenor House on Park Lane. A bit beyond my means but where there's a will there's a way. Both hotels were popular venues for corporate cocktail parties, once a year knees-ups for their clients, suppliers or sales forces. The trick was to choose big events where the welcoming line of big cheeses clasped the guests warmly by the hand but knew them not personally. And so it came to pass, warm greetings, even congratulations on our sales figures for the Magic Mop or Supa Suds and my flat mate and I were liberated into the throng where trays of tepid wine, vol-au-vents, pineapple and cheese on sticks and sticky cocktail sausages were circulating. We just had to avoid all eye contact so others didn't join us for a discussion on the joys of working for Magic Mop. Replete, we nodded our thanks to the hosts and departed. Also QED. Today, Security would probably have us handcuffed and in a Black Maria before you could say vol-au-vent.

The rent was £9 a week between the four of us. Today rented flats in Queen's Gate cost £1,000 a week or more. We were lucky to live in a time when we could afford a favoured part of London, albeit in shabby style, as the now seriously upmarket South Ken is beyond all but the fattest bank accounts.

The Swinging Sixties were still a few years away and I suppose our lives were rather dull in comparison to what we would later enthusiastically embrace. But we were happy enough. The food was dire: I remember cooking endless spaghetti bolognese and buying endless Fray Bentos steak and kidney pies in a tin. However long I cooked them, the pastry was always soggy, the thought of which now turns my stomach! I was surprised to see that it's still on the supermarket shelves. Our clothes were dire too. Some we made ourselves, horror of horrors, often turning out some hideous garment in one evening. We were always skint, and, unless we struck lucky, dates consisted of a couple of halves of IPA in the pub, from which we were shooed out at 10 p.m. by the landlord clanging a bell and proclaiming 'Time, *gentlemen*, please.' Apparently, ladies didn't drink in pubs. The only place you could get a drink after ten was the then airline terminal in Cromwell Road, to which we sometimes repaired. On the plus side, you could see Laurence Olivier on the live stage for half a crown (12½p) up in the gods and park your car outside the theatre.

We would sometimes go to the Saturday night 'hop' at Chelsea Old Town Hall, the thought of which now is cringe-making. It was mainly ballroom dancing with an orchestra. We would tart ourselves up in the hope of meeting a trendy boy, but there were no trendy boys and it was all pretty grim. The girls in their posh frocks – perish the thought of jeans and trainers – would sit around, waiting to be asked to dance. I wasn't a great success. When I was asked, which was not very often, by the time I had uncoiled myself from my seat to my full 5'11" height, most boys had scarpered. They all seemed to be vertically challenged; there was usually a glut of 5'6" boys. I wasn't going to find my Mr Right there, nor, happily, did I want to, but my flatmate Frances did – she and Peter met under the revolving glitterball and have clocked up many years of wedded bliss.

Job-wise, having cut my teeth at a newspaper, I wanted to continue in something creative. I'd discovered enough about PR, still in its infancy, for it to appeal and it played to my creative side. It was the next best thing to journalism. The quickest way was to get a secretarial job with a PR company and learn the ropes that way. I couldn't have asked for a better intro. Just turned twenty-one I found a job at FJ Lyons, a consultancy in South Kensington where I shared an office with my two bosses, Tony Moorhouse and David Bland, experienced at their craft and delightful to work for. We worked on just one huge account: the Australian Food and Wine Industry Board, which broke down into five smaller boards encompassing wine, meat, wool, fresh fruit and dried fruit. Gradually, I took on more responsibility and learnt a lot during my two years there.

I may have found my niche but my hoped-for future career would have to wait. The travel bug had bitten. Hard.

CHAPTER 3

HELLO UNCLE SAM

I yearned to go to the mighty USA, the Land of Milk and Honey, as it was then. Intrepid I might have been, but it didn't extend to solo travelling for a couple of years. I needed a companion. This turned out to be not that easy, as not everyone wants to drop everything for the unknown thousands of miles away. Furthermore, compatibility was important. Sally, my school friend and flatmate, was up for it … until she inconveniently (from my point of view) met the man she was to marry (albeit not for long).

'I'm sure Margaret will go with you,' she said, well aware that Margaret was boring.

'Not a good suggestion,' I retorted. 'I was thinking of someone more dynamic'.

Margaret had also been at my school but we hadn't had much to do with each other. She was always a bit of a loner. She was a good cello player but was rather dull. Not that I'd set the Thames on fire myself, but I had serious doubts about how we'd get along. Yet there was no rush from others to fill the vacancy and time was getting short. And so, Margaret became my travelling companion for two years. I needn't have worried. Our different personalities appeared not to bother her and she morphed into a happy, funny and engaging companion during our American adventure, and we got on fine without any fallouts. Out went the mouse and in came Miss Personality Plus, and she was popular wherever she went.

It was the first of my three Atlantic, one Pacific and two South Atlantic crossings by liner, sadly now a thing of the past. It was a wonderful way to travel and the Dutch-owned Statendam was a splendid ship, even in steerage. That first crossing was probably the best because of the sheer exhilaration of six days on an ocean liner, a romance with the third engineer, and the breathtaking sight of the Statue of Liberty as dawn broke over New York's harbour. Margaret and I were both choked with excitement as we stepped onto American soil.

Hello Uncle Sam.

Sixties America was a fascinating decade. It was the dawn of a golden age and the election of the handsome and charismatic Jack Kennedy enhanced its status, as did his wife, Jacqueline, a beautiful and socially adept first lady. It was a time of contrasts. On the one hand, there was the Civil Rights Movement, the Vietnam War and women fighting for equal rights; on the other, opulence and indulgence. The opulent America was the one, to my shame, I was more aware of and I loved its flamboyance and excesses. To me, it was a glorious culture shock after the austerity we were experiencing in England, where we were still recovering from the War and rationing had only relatively recently been withdrawn. By the end of the decade, the Vietnam War was raging on, Jack Kennedy and his brother Robert had been assassinated as had the Civil Rights Leader, Martin Luther 'I Have a Dream' King.

Chicago fitted the bill as far as prosperity was concerned. Everyone seemed well off, the shops were ritzy and glitzy, the cars stretched forever. While our boyfriends back home had jalopies if we were lucky, our dates in the

US had convertible Cadillacs. Chicago was humming and we got stuck into everything it had to offer. With soaring skyscrapers and Lake Michigan alongside it, it was an attractive second city and a good place to cut our American teeth.

Our arrival hadn't been without glitches. I'd gone through an agent in London to get my green card – not a problem as it was a status symbol to have a British secretary with 'that cute little English accent' – and she, a charming woman I'd thought, had also fixed me up with a job and arranged accommodation for Margaret and me. Mercifully, the green card and accommodation were genuine but the job didn't exist. It was a sham. Not such a charming woman.

With only a few dollars to my name, I needed to find work immediately. Thankfully, it was easy and because an excellent salary was offered – $400 a month, equivalent to £532 then – I found myself working for an insurance company. Lubin & Lubin was another eye opener. It had a state-of-the-art office with every mod con from electric pencil sharpeners to the latest electric typewriters and pre-carbonised paper for any copies that had to be made. The Lubins loved me, not for my secretarial skills but for that cute English accent. With my arrival, telephone calls had to be channelled through me and I heard one caller saying to my boss, 'Gee, Bob, can you get me one of those?' They were most displeased when I gave in my notice.

Our accommodation was at the Eleanor Parkway Club in North Dearborn Parkway Street, known, for good reason, as the Virgins' Retreat. It was a respectable establishment for nice young ladies, not quite our scene but suited us well enough at that time, as everything was provided, including breakfast and dinner every day. Suitably attired gentlemen callers were allowed but only in the communal room, and there was a strict curfew.

Our two-year plan had been to split the months between three cities. Chicago and San Francisco were our first choices and the third was chosen with a pin in the map. We came up with Denver, one of the gold-prospecting towns in the Wild West in the mid-19th century. As it happened, Denver got short-changed as we decided to extend our time in Chicago and San Francisco and Denver was reduced to a few weeks.

Just a week or two before our departure from Chicago I met a gorgeous man, a doctor called Tom, and I often wonder what might have happened had I stayed on.

'Can't you just delay your departure for a few weeks so we can see if this relationship is going anywhere?' he suggested.

I wasn't in the marriage market then (or for many years to come) but this was a *coup de foudre* for us both, so who knows? I rejected his suggestion as I had Margaret to consider, we'd already given in our notice at work and the Virgins' Retreat, and it seemed the sensible, right thing to do. I'm not sure that besotted twenty-two-year-olds are supposed to be sensible but I stuck with it. It was one of those 'sliding doors' moments that get a good airing in this book: the choices we have and the decisions we make for better or worse. How different my life would have been as a Chicago housewife if the relationship had stood the test of time. Would I be making pumpkin pie for Halloween and taking my turn as chairperson of the Chicago Foundation for Women? Hmm. Not my bag!

Apart from it giving me constant nose bleeds because of the altitude, the Mile-High City of Denver was an enjoyable interlude. Its setting against the mighty Rockies was spectacular, and it was a friendly, relatively small town. Margaret and I found temporary secretarial jobs to bring in some bucks and stayed at a spectacular short-term apartment with a walk-in wardrobe and refrigerator and every kitchen gadget known to man. A happy change of scene after the Virgins' Retreat.

While in Denver we bought a car, an elderly Chevrolet station wagon, but there was a snag: I couldn't drive. Margaret already had a UK driving licence and when she found she just had to go round the block to pass her Colorado test, she persuaded me to have a go. The car was automatic so I jerkily manoeuvred it round the block with the examiner and awaited the verdict.

'I've passed you,' he said, as if not believing it himself, 'but you would do well to remember that we drive on the right-hand side of the road in America.'

And there I was, a newly fledged driver. It was an interesting milestone; the start of delivering cars all over the country. During two periods in North America, this rookie went on to clock up about 25,000 miles travelling through forty of the fifty states and a good stretch of Canada.

There were many happy times during our American adventure but San Francisco was, without doubt, the best. It was pre-Haight-Ashbury, the bohemian hangout in the late sixties, a retreat for hippies and flower power – but it already had a whiff of what was to come. It was a magical city with its quirky architecture, the Golden Gate Bridge, cable cars coping with the steepest of hills, Fisherman's Wharf, music, a wide variety of night-life including the legendary hungry i – it had it all and on the other side of the Golden Gate Bridge were the waterside villages of Sausalito and Tiburon

I was twenty-three. What better age to enjoy its bounty?

We were delighted with our quirky apartment on Scott and Clay – a loft which suited San Francisco and was very different from the state-of-the-art Denver flat – and we were soon joined by Brenda, a friend from the UK newly arrived in the States. Brenda was stunning: a Jackie Kennedy lookalike, which did her no harm. She was also as vain as they come but laughed at herself for it, had a delightful personality and soon became one of my best friends.[2]

I don't recall how I met American John and his pals, Englishman Roger and German Heinz, but the six of us made a jolly group. Most weekends we would drive to Lake Berryessa in the Napa Valley, eighty-odd miles northeast of the city, and set up camp by the huge lake. Visitors flock to Lake Berryessa in their thousands now, but we rarely saw anyone else.

It was idyllic, the sun always shone, which it certainly didn't do in San Francisco, and we slept under the stars, tents soon being discarded. We water-skied – thanks to John's speedboat – swam, barbecued, drank beer and put the world to rights as one does at that age. As far as I personally was concerned, the world was in damn good shape right then. In fact, it was heaven and I still have very special memories of those days more than sixty years later.

Bombing up and down State Route 1 – the highway that runs along 656 miles of the Pacific coastline – was another favourite pursuit. We'd stop off in Monterey (whenever I hear Dave Brubeck's 'Take Five' I am transported back to the Monterey Jazz Festival) or Carmel, Big Sur or even

2 Cancer claimed Brenda prematurely in her sixties, far too young for such a vital and energetic person. I still miss her a lot. Her daughter Zoë is my cherished goddaughter.

drive all the way to LA.

Far too soon it was time to go home. The parents had summoned me back for the weddings of both my brothers, Brenda was going to stay in New York for a while and Margaret was off to the West Indies. It was time to say goodbye to John and Co. I kept in touch with John for a while but that soon lapsed. About six years ago, I thought it would be fun to see if I could track him down. Success: his champion fencer status was the key Google needed to come up trumps. He hadn't moved far – just to Oregon, California's northern neighbour. We were delighted to be in touch again fifty-five years on and now, both of us octogenarians, text each other on Messenger every day.

Back to 1963, and we needed to find a car to get us to New York or thereabouts. The only one we could find to deliver that way was a tiny Peugeot, which we had to take to Boston, a distance of some 3,000 miles. We were given a time limit of twelve days. Fortunately for us, the mileage was not recorded so we were able to go off-piste, quite a bit off-piste, and we clocked up 5,000 miles.

It was an epic journey, three of us packed into a tiny car with all our clobber. We drove through fourteen states and to give us time to see the sights, we sometimes drove through the night, otherwise we stopped at a motel. Despite the time restriction we managed to gamble in Las Vegas, descend the Grand Canyon and even drop down way south to jazz it up in New Orleans. From there it was straight up the Eastern Seaboard to Boston.

After safely delivering the car to its own parking slot at Boston's Brandeis University, we went back to New York on a Greyhound bus. Margaret then went off to the West Indies, and Brenda and I, now both strapped for cash (again), booked into a dollar-a-night place in West 88th. She was waiting to move into an apartment with some American girls for a few months and I needed to get a temporary job for three weeks to pay for my sea journey home. Brenda spent her time in her bug-eaten bed in the filthy doss house as she got flu, but I was able to escape during the day to the glamour of a Park Avenue office for yet another temp secretarial job. I must have been crawling with bed bugs and the like; I wonder if they took up residence in Park Avenue…

CHAPTER 4

HOME TO THE BIG FREEZE

by Sylvia

It was tough arriving back in England in 1963 when the country was experiencing the Big Freeze, one of the coldest winters on record. Snow was still banked up high on either side of the road and our family house in Bristol had no central heating. It was freezing. Get me back to America!

Instead, off I went to London again where there were compensations to come – the Swinging Sixties would soon be swinging into life. The music revolution had already arrived: the Beatles; the Rolling Stones; big-haired, kohl-eyed Dusty Springfield; bare-footed Sandie Shaw and many more whose music and lyrics have stood the test of time. It was then time for the fashion explosion. One minute we were dressed like our mothers, the next we were in Mary Quant miniskirts, Courrèges boots and Vidal Sassoon haircuts. I was never a beauty but I had a good pair of pins so miniskirts and, a bit later, hotpants, were just the ticket for me

Carnaby Street and the Kings Road came alive, and Biba opened its first shop in Abingdon Road, a residential street in Kensington, finally taking over the whole of Derry & Tom's department store. London had morphed from a gloomy, post-war capital into the epicentre of youth culture, full of style, hope and promise. And fun.

The Swinging Sixties explosion aside, the contrast between America and Great Britain was vast in those days. My standards honed in America needed to plummet, particularly when it came to accommodation and cars. Although our Chevy station wagon wasn't in the first flush of youth, it was positively flash compared to what I could now afford: a 1938 Morris Eight which cost me £35. I should have kept it as it would be worth five figures now.

It was a great little motor. It invariably needed to be cranked into life, its brakes were almost non-existent and the indicators shot out of the side of the vehicle – or didn't. Needless to say, it had no heating and some of the floor was missing. Mercifully, no MOTs were required in those days. My happiest memories in my Morris Eight were the monthly weekend visits back to the family home in Bristol with pals whose families also lived in Bristol. There was no motorway then, so our journey was via the A4. There were plenty of pubs en route, and no drinking and driving rules back then, so we would invariably stop off in Newbury and Chippenham, and maybe Reading and Malmesbury. It wasn't so much that we were irresponsible, more that it never occurred to us that sobriety when driving was a good idea. We weren't alone.

I don't remember any breakdowns on those trips, but the AA certainly earned its fees over the years. I'm talking about the Automobile Association, not the other AA – but that might have come in handy after our pub crawls along the A4. In the early sixties, the patrolmen rode motorbikes with a sidecar and they saluted all car drivers who were displaying AA badges on the front of their cars. Keep your eyes on the badges rather than the road!

Despite London's renaissance, rented accommodation

was still pretty bad. Bristol friend, Jenny, newly escaped from a hideous marriage, and I found a basement flat in Tregunter Road in Earls Court, and we advertised in the *Evening Standard* for a third sharer. Such ads always attracted a massive response, but the paper published the wrong telephone number. Astute Sally, already a successful Fleet Street journalist at the age of twenty-one, rang the newspaper to find out the correct number and, with no competition, claimed the cupboard of a room on offer. We became close friends and remain so to this day.

I soon found my first job as a bona fide PR person with Bowater Scott, the disposable paper manufacturers that made Andrex and Scottie tissues. I even had my own secretary and a company car.

It was the ideal place to learn about what others have described as the 'dark arts'. PR often gets a bad press; spin doctors are blamed for all kinds of dreadful behaviour, but it's a career that I have found suits my personality to perfection. Apart from all the PR nuts and bolts – press releases, photocalls, press conferences, media and reputation management, brand development and so on, it's a catch-all for so many other things – if there's not an obvious answer or someone able to do something difficult, pass it to PR. You need creativity to find newsworthy ideas in prosaic places and also writing skills to ghostwrite clients' articles, comment pieces and speeches. Confidence and a sense of humour help too and even sewing skills, as I was to find at Bowater Scott.

Disposable paper products for hospitals were gaining interest in the fight against cross infection and Bowater Scott was the leader of the pack, promoting their use for medical purposes and in industry. National newspapers and medical journals were my target and demonstrations of the safety of a variety of disposable items were held in teaching hospitals. There were also press visits to their new state-of-the-art factory in Northfleet. They weren't invited to the ancient factory in Walthamstow, straight out of the industrial revolution! The consumer side was more flippant and gave me rein for some good photo calls. Brand leader Andrex and Scottie tissues were their main domestic lines. Loo paper had come a long way since Bronco[3] days and now the company was introducing patterned Andrex. The just released film of the much-lauded musical *My Fair Lady* was the talk of the town and from a swathe of the paper from the factory, I copied one of Cecil Beaton's glamorous Edwardian-style dresses created for Audrey Hepburn. It was modelled by my secretary, Andy, at the photo call who did a good job but given the publicity it created, I should have hired an Audrey Hepburn lookalike. I was still on that to-be-avoided expression 'learning curve'.

Soon after I left the company in 1966, it was swallowed up by Kimberly Clark, the Kleenex people.

Bowater House occupied an enviable position in Knightsbridge overlooking Hyde Park. So enviable, in fact, that some years later it was razed to the ground and One Hyde Park, the world's most expensive residential block, rose up in its place at a cost of £1.15 billion. It has eighty-six apartments, the cheapest selling for around the £20 million mark. The most expensive is the £160 million penthouse, complete with its own swimming pool, cinema and library. What exalted a space I once occupied to write humble press releases.

3 Single sheets of hard, shiny, non-absorbent lavatory paper.

1963 was also the year of the Profumo sex scandal, the Great Train Robbery and, sadly, the assassination of President Kennedy.

The Profumo affair had all the ingredients to keep the country mesmerised for months – a disgraced Secretary of State for War, call girls, a Soviet naval attaché suspected of being a spy and a society osteopath and socialite. It brought the Conservative government to its knees and defeat at the next election and, tragically, the osteopath Stephen Ward committed suicide during the final stage of his trial which found him guilty of immorality offences. John Profumo dedicated the rest of his working life to Toynbee Hall, a charity for the many deprived people living in dreadful conditions in the East End of London.

The Great Train Robbery had much of the country cheering the robbers for pulling off such a remarkable heist without a shot being fired: £2.6 million from a Royal Mail train travelling from Glasgow to London. The cheering subsided when it emerged that the train driver had been beaten over the head and was never able to work again.

No one whose memory goes back to 22 November 1963 will ever forget where they were on that shattering day when President Kennedy was assassinated. I was on a number 14 bus on my way to a supper party in Putney. At the Harrods stop a passenger getting on the bus blurted out the terrible news. Kennedy's death shook the world. I'd been back from America only a few months and felt an almost personal loss at his death. I was still in love with everything American and the glamorous and vital president had been a big part of my life there. It was difficult to believe he was dead. The horrific scenes of him being shot and dying as the stunned Jackie Kennedy, her pink Chanel suit soaked in blood, climbed onto the back of the car to retrieve fragments of her husband's skull, will stay with me forever.

CHAPTER 5

FROM CANADA TO HONG KONG

by Sylvia

The travel bug was nagging and I couldn't resist another foray when a London friend Jean, suggested going to Canada for a few months and then on to Hong Kong. I was interested to see how Canada matched up to its big brother neighbour where I had spent two happy years. We plumped for Vancouver on the West Coast. People rave about this beautiful city, but in 1966 we found it a dull place, quite different from Seattle, the lively US city just over the border.

Jean and I rented a scruffy apartment where we were joined by Anna, a schoolfriend of Jean, and the three of us got on famously. Anna, blessed with brains and beauty, was funny and a clever mimic, and Jean was equally excellent company.

I was back with my old friend the typewriter to earn a crust and my job in Vancouver was with a mining company which was drilling for oil in Alberta. They were positive they were close to a major strike, so positive that all my spare cash went into it. This included the dollars I earned moonlighting a couple of times a week as an unlikely hostess in a 'night club', aka a soulless barn where the clientele had to be seated at all times while the hostesses served them drinks. We wore the most hideous slinky gold lurex gowns which had hosted many occupants but never seen a dry cleaner. Five-star hotels and the barns were the only place to drink in 1966 Vancouver, and alcohol to take away was available only in bottle shops during restricted hours.

Together with a few million others situated around the world, I remember us watching a football match on 30 July 1966 on our small and flickering black-and-white television. The commentator, Kenneth Wolstenholme, wrote his name into sporting history with the famous line 'They think it's all over – it is now' as England clinched victory over West Germany in the 1966 World Cup.

An unexpected and exciting letter arrived for me from Hong Kong from Angela Quinn, a one-time PR manager at Bowater Scott, my erstwhile place of work. She was an account executive at Galitzine Marklin, the leading PR company in Hong Kong, and she'd written to offer me her job as she was going back to the UK. She explained that I'd have to see the directors on arrival, but assured me the job was mine if I wanted it. This was thrilling news; my typing fingers could again be put to rest and my creative hat donned. The news speeded up Jean's and my departure from Vancouver and Anna was happily going to Toronto to stay with cousins.

We needed to get to San Francisco to pick up our transport to Hong Kong, the SS President Wilson. We hopped over to Seattle where, of course, we picked up a car for delivery to San Francisco, a distance of some 800 miles on Highway 101 through Washington, Oregon and northern California. The scenery was quite spectacular – a wild and rugged coast and magnificent trees including the massive Redwoods. It was – it is – outstandingly beautiful.

We set sail in December 1966 on a three-week journey across the Pacific Ocean with a stopover in Hawaii.

Sailing into Hong Kong harbour in the early morning sunshine was thrilling and it also meant liberation from the quite appalling ship. Steerage was a kind word for our accommodation – so different from my Atlantic crossings. The inside cabins were miniscule, the food was horrible, the passengers' lounge was basic and the entertainment non-existent. To add insult to injury my 'not wanted on voyage' baggage, consigned to the ship's hold, had been sitting in water in the porous hold throughout the crossing.

There was a letter from Galitzine Marklin awaiting me on my arrival, fixing a meeting that very day. I could hardly take it all in; so much was happening. The two directors who saw me sounded positive.

'That's great, Sylvia,' one of them told me. 'We're sure you'll fit in very well with our team. All we need now is for you to sign the contract.' He pushed the document across the table.

I looked at the contract and it stared back at me. What was that? The small print included a five-year commitment to stay with Galitzine Marklin! No expat terms were offered and it seemed a stiff stipulation as I had no intention of staying in Hong Kong for so long (or so I thought at the time). The upshot was that I lost the job. Should I have lied and sworn unswerving devotion to Galitzine Marklin? Maybe. In the rush of the moment I felt I'd be letting Angela down if I signed and then reneged. She later told me no one kept to the terms, but by then it was too late.

It was a bitter blow but at least I knew that all the money I had invested in my Vancouver employer's dead cert oil well would by now be gushing with liquid gold. I hot-footed it to Post Restante for the expected telegram. It was there all right.

A millionaire you are not. Coming up with water.

Welcome to Hong Kong, Sylvia. So much for Day One.

Jean had also invested in the oil well, so we were both now in rather a pitiful financial state. Again! In fact, the well did finally produce oil, lashings and lashings of it, and our shares multiplied many times. But there's another twist. I had entrusted my shares to a 'friend' – a colleague at the mining company – asking him to act for me when instructed. As the stock went up and up, he took the liberty of selling them to himself. Nice friend. It was one of a few occasions when my trust in people went seriously wrong. However, for better or worse I continue my belief, as I'm sure people respond positively to being trusted.

With no job and the oil well producing water we needed to find cheap accommodation and Chungking Mansions in Kowloon's Nathan Road was certainly very cheap – and nasty. Anyone who knows Hong Kong will know Chungking Mansions, a labyrinth of passages with stalls selling tat on the ground floor and numerous rickety lifts rising to a variety of dubious guest houses, rooms and flats, many of them brothels. While much of today's Hong Kong is unrecognisable from my day, on a recent trip there I was pleased to see that Chungking Mansions hadn't been gentrified. I hope that's still the case.

My next task was to find a job. It took little time to discover that as PR was in its infancy in Hong Kong, jobs were few and far between. No matter, back to the faithful typewriter. Except nobody wanted me to type either. We had arrived at the beginning of the Hong Kong riots in

1967 between the Chinese Pro-Communists – the Cultural Revolution under Chairman Mao was in full swing – and the Hong Kong government, defending British colonial rule.

It was not a good time for *gweilos*, the Cantonese word for 'foreign devils', and companies were not keen to employ a British girl. Each day I would start at the top of a skyscraper of offices and work my way down, seeking any work anyone could offer. To no avail. Jean managed to get a good job with the Hong Kong and Shanghai Bank, so at least some money was coming in. Finally, the big import/export company Hutchinsons offered me the position as secretary to the accountant. It was music to my ears and a great relief to get anything, even accountancy, but when asked if I could start the next day, I demurred and said it would have to be the following one.

Why, when I was so desperate did I do that? What an extraordinary thing to do, there was no rhyme or reason for the delay.

Except there was a very big reason; a very big 'sliding doors' moment. I didn't know it then but the next day I was invited for an interview at The Peninsula Hotel, the *grande dame* of the Far East and one of the top five hotels in the world. So began five – yes, five! – of some of the happiest years of my life.

My job was secretary to the Food and Beverage Manager, Bruno Dedual, and we instantly became fast and firm platonic friends – a friendship which endured until his death. We had lots of jolly times in Hong Kong and enjoyed holidays in a good few other places around the world.

The Peninsula, or the Pen as it is always known, was a simply wonderful place to work in those days before the bottom line became the only calculation as to the success of a company. I loved every moment of it but thought I'd blown it when, still in the early days, I won a beer-drinking contest (speed, not quantity) in a local bar. To my horror, my photo and a write-up mentioning the Pen appeared on the front page of the next day's *South China Morning Post*. Not very seemly for a Pen employee. Was I for the chop?

I didn't have to wait long to find out: one of the little white-uniformed page boys arrived in our office bearing a bottle of beer on a silver tray 'With the compliments of the General Manager'. I didn't know the Big Chief well then as it was still early days, but my beer-drinking exploit seemed to break the ice and from then on we had an excellent relationship.

The hotel was certainly posh and inevitably elitist. But it had a soul, possibly because, unlike five-star London hotels, it was frequented by the locals, albeit well-heeled ones. 'Where East meets West' was the name given to the vast lobby, a popular watering hole for both Chinese and Western residents.

The Great and the Good stayed there, of course, including a lot of showbiz's A list: Frank Sinatra, Bing Crosby, Noël Coward, Danny Kaye, etc. What was extraordinary was the number of well-known people who stole things. Ashtray nicking was still stealing but had become acceptable (and the ashtrays were cheap for that reason); the bedsheets, towelling robes and *objets d'art* were not. The General Manager was once tipped off by the room boy that a well-known international financier checking out of his suite had removed a huge oval silver tray on which his breakfast had been served. The GM hurried to reception, which was part of the busy lobby, greeted the thief warmly with a slap on his back and crash, bang, down came the tray from underneath the man's jacket, much to the bemusement of all in attendance.

Jean and I soon escaped the squalor of Chungking Mansions and moved to a more salubrious flat in MacDonnell Road on Hong Kong Island, which entailed the peerless commute to Kowloon across the harbour on the Star Ferry. The island was nervy sometimes as the riots were gathering pace. I remember returning there on a boiling hot Saturday afternoon to the sound of serious trouble close by. As my taxi took me around the cricket field adjacent to the riots in full swing, the sound of leather on willow and 'Good shot, old boy' pervaded the air.

Today's Hong Kong is unrecognisable from my time, which was before any reclamation of land and before any tunnels between Kowloon and Hong Kong Island. The only way across the Harbour was by Star Ferry, a *wallah wallah* (a small motor boat) at night time and the vehicular ferry, the only means of transporting a car from one side to the other. I used the vehicular ferry from time to time to take Fred, my much-treasured TR3, for a spin around the island.

When Bruno was due to go on three months' leave, much to my astonishment I was offered the job as Acting Food and Beverage Manager. I'm sure some of those heading up other departments – all Swiss, all men and all graduates of the prestigious *Ecole Hôtelière de Lausanne* – must have raised an eyebrow or two and wondered how an Englishwoman with no hotel qualifications could have landed such a job. As indeed did I, but all of them were ready to help me and did. I survived my tenure, and on Bruno's return I became Assistant F&B Manager.

Then came the problem I had been dreading. My

travel plans with Jean had not reckoned on a long-term stay in Hong Kong and we'd planned to take some time trekking overland to the UK. I couldn't bear the thought of leaving, but didn't feel I could let her down. Reluctantly, I gave in my notice. A juicy carrot was dangled in front of me if I stayed on. I would be given a two-year expat contract which meant a free flat, paid leave, fares paid home, substantial perks and the job of Banqueting Manager. Luckily, Jean found another companion, leaving me free to stay on for two more wonderful years. The glass ceiling got a crack as I was the first woman and non-Swiss to be given an expat contract.

Interestingly and most encouragingly, albeit many years later, the glass ceiling was well and truly shattered as the present General Manager is a Chinese woman.

CHAPTER 6

TROPICAL SPRUE IN KATHMANDU

by Sylvia

When my time for overseas leave came round I decided to hop in and out of a dozen countries en route back to England. This time I was travelling solo and enjoying the freedom. I can't call it backpacking as, unbelievably, I carted a couple of suitcases with no wheels around the world! There were no mod cons like mobile phones, Google or ATMs – or even backpacks as we know them today.

It's sad to look back and see that since my 1969 trip, five of the countries I visited have been war-torn: Cambodia, Myanmar (then Burma), Afghanistan, India's Kashmir and Lebanon's Beirut.

Burma was closed off to the rest of the world except for transient travellers who were allowed to stay for a maximum of twenty-four hours. I stayed at the Strand Hotel in Rangoon, as it was then, which was trying desperately to keep up the standards of its glorious colonial past. Starched white tablecloths and napkins, albeit darned, adorned the table in the once beautiful dining room and the gallant three-piece orchestra played to a virtually empty room, Titanic style. Happily, the hotel is now back to its former glory.

The exchange rate from American dollars to the Burmese kyat was prohibitive and although an excellent rate was available on the black market, I was warned against it. If caught, I wouldn't be seeing my homeland for some time. I wanted to see the famous gold-plated Shwedagon Pagoda with its diamond-studded spire, so I walked as I had no money for transport. Getting there was easy, the Pagoda being clearly visible, but I got lost on my way back to the hotel and it was beginning to get dark. I asked a couple of young men for directions and they insisted on walking all the way to the hotel with me. I asked them to wait while I fetched some dollars from my room to thank them, but they refused.

'It has been our pleasure to help a visitor to our country,' they said.

The Burmese seemed to be a delightful and peaceful race. Alas, history tells us otherwise.

Kathmandu was next on the itinerary and, as to be expected at some time on such a journey, Delhi Belly came a-calling. It was no big deal apart from making me queasy on and off for the rest of my trip, and I lost a lot of weight.

Last stop Paris, where I enjoyed a couple of complimentary nights at the George V Hotel. It was an unwritten understanding between the management of five-star hotels around the world that they would offer each other free accommodation. The 'old boy' network put me up in luxury at the Phoenicia in Beirut and the Grande Bretagne in Athens. The Oriental in Bangkok also obliged. George V's General Manager, a Maurice Chevalier-style charmer and his equally charming wife took me on a great night out in wonderful Paris, a fitting end to my travels.

And at last to the motherland, where I wasted no time in seeking medical help as by this time Delhi Belly had rendered me skeletal. No wonder. It turned out that I was suffering from a nasty tropical disease with the unlikely name of Tropical Sprue. I languished in the Tropical Diseases Hospital in London for three weeks, and it was there that I heard the immortal words spoken for the first time 'One giant leap for mankind' as Neil Armstrong stepped onto the surface of the moon. I also watched Ann Haydon Jones win Wimbledon. My companions, who were cheerful lepers, and I watched it on a minute television in the dayroom.

Sprue patients were rare in the hospital so I was much sought after for the tropical medicine students to diagnose my complaint. I got ten bob for every session! If they asked me to stick my tongue out, I knew they were on to it, as mine was covered in spots, a giveaway in its diagnosis. The disease had been considered dangerous with many deaths until humble folic acid was found to be its saviour.

The hospital told me I must remain in a temperate climate for the rest of my life, as Sprue flourishes in the tropics and subtropics. This ruled Hong Kong out. I went back anyway and am still alive more than fifty years later. I have to admit that it took me several years to rid myself completely of it and still avoid very rich food cooked with cream. I enjoyed another happy two years at the Pen but then it was decision time – another attractive contract was on the table or should I return to reality? When the pros and cons were added up, I decided it was time to go home. Sometime later I was honoured to receive The Peninsula's Distinguished Alumnus Award.

When I set sail from Southampton, the intention had been to be away for two years. I'd overstayed by four years. London awaited. Were my travelling days over at last?

CHAPTER 7

BACK TO THE MOTHERLAND

by Sylvia

Although I missed Hong Kong, it was exciting to be back in London. Still, I needed to adjust after my pampered lifestyle at the Pen. In Hong Kong, my bed was made every day with clean sheets, towels changed, washing done and food and drink delivered to the fridge as per my daily shopping list. Even Room Service would oblige, a waiter trotting along Nathan Road to my flat in the Lane Crawford building, a pole over his shoulder bearing my dinner.

Time to get real. This time I intended to stay in much-loved London and put down roots. The two most important things to do were to buy a flat – my first dalliance with the world of property – and a good long-term job. As it happened, they both fell into my lap. A recently converted two-bedroomed flat in Camden Park Road in north London suited me well and cost just £7,350. It was a snip even in 1972. And the Carlton Tower hotel in Knightsbridge just happened to be looking for a PR Manager, a job which was tailormade for me.

There is always something special about the first property you own and this was no different for me. The sitting room walls were smothered in pictures I'd picked up on my travels, and I went into full OTT mode in my bedroom. Laura Ashley was all the rage at that time and a flowery blue wallpaper from her collection covered every wall. I made a bedspread from the same fabric for the bed and the to-the-ground tablecloths for the round bedside tables. Definitely overkill! I loved the flat and had no plans to move, but when my neighbours above me announced they were selling, I snapped up their property before it went on the market and moved upstairs. The flat was bright and spacious, and best of all it had a splendid secluded roof terrace. Of all the flats I later bought and sold as a sideline business, this was my favourite.

The Carlton Tower, situated on Sloane Street and close to all the delights of Knightsbridge (at a price) had had several owners and it had just been taken over by Lex Garages when I arrived on the scene as their PR Manager, a strange bedfellow for a luxury hotel.

As well as the usual mixed bag of PR responsibilities - press releases, photo opportunities, think tanks for marketing opportunities, promotions and the rest, I always enjoyed the entertaining side, which included the press and celebrity guests. Some celebs were charming companions, others could be very hard work. One such was Tennessee Williams. The great playwright had a way with words but he was no conversationalist and although I could usually get through such occasions with small talk, not this time, and it was a relief when our awkward tea came to an end. Not my finest hour or probably half hour – he escaped sharpish!

David Niven was more fun and lived up to his handsome and debonair image when shooting the film *Vampira* at the Carlton Tower – he played Count Dracula.

Chris Bonington and his co-mountaineers on their way back from their Everest expedition in 1972 held their press conference at the hotel. The press turned up in droves to laud them even though they had *failed* to get to the top of the world's highest mountain (they made it in 1975). In the 70s it was still rare for anyone to scale it, half way up was laudable, not laughable. Now mountaineers are almost queuing to make the ascent and around 7000 have.

The PR managers of some of London's top hotels, including the Dorchester, Savoy, Ritz and Grosvenor House, would get together for a lunch each month, taking it in turns to host the event. We had a pleasant lunch at the Lancaster Gate Hotel, hosted by Barbara Harris, who announced she would be leaving soon to get married. She didn't mention to whom: she became the fifth and last wife of Cary Grant. She had met him when he stayed at the hotel for a sponsored event. No such luck for me at the Carlton Tower.

The previous owner of the hotel was the American group, Sonesta, who decided to change the hotel's name to Sonesta Tower. Bad move. Carlton Tower has a certain cachet; Sonesta Tower could have been a B&B in Southend. The hotel lost guests in droves. The bed linen, towels, cutlery, plates and glasses had all been changed to bear the Sonesta Tower imprint. Back they went to the Carlton Tower. The cost must have been exorbitant.

I'd now been back in the metropolis for two years without any sign of itchy feet. I was happy in my flat, had a good social life and was enjoying working at the hotel where I knew I was doing a good job. But beware the new broom. In came a new General Manager and out I went. He didn't last long but long enough to give me and countless others our marching orders. He was hellbent on redundancies to make his balance sheet look good and didn't even wait to see who was expendable. To add insult to injury, my dismissal was just inside the two-year redundancy laws. It occurred to me that had I been there for another couple of weeks my position might have been safe. Huge injustice for me and others but there was nowt we could do. We were out.

CHAPTER 8

DAYLIGHT ROBBERY IN SOUTH AFRICA

by Sylvia

Unceremoniously dumped by the Carlton Tower with no redundancy money, I needed to find employment quickly. The end of 1973 was not a good time to be job hunting as Britain was in the throes of the three-day week imposed by the Prime Minister, Edward Heath, to conserve power. The fuel crisis in the Middle East had seen the price of petrol quadruple, if you could find any, and the miners' strike resulted in a serious shortage of electricity, which mostly came from coal in those days. It was a miserable time: in Piccadilly Circus, all shop windows and many lamp posts were unlit, most pubs were closed, no heating was allowed in shops, offices or restaurants, the BBC and ITV alternated nightly and had to close down at 10.30. Even the weather was horrible.

I didn't have much hope of getting a job I wanted, given the dire situation the country was in, yet I was adamant I wanted to stay in the hotel industry and at the top level, natch. Such jobs were not plentiful and the Harrods PR Manager pipped me at the post for the one vacancy there was, at the newly built InterContinental Hotel on the corner of Hyde Park Corner and Park Lane. I don't doubt the right decision was made as her Harrods experience and little black book of addresses would have been a great plus.

I finally decided to escape the horrors of London, satisfy the last vestiges of my travel bug and get a bit of sunshine. A previous Carlton Tower executive, by then a big shot with Southern Sun Hotels in South Africa, was on the lookout for people with UK hotel experience so I had no problem being taken on. It was during apartheid but I wanted to see for myself what it was like and off I went again on the mail ship RMS Edinburgh Castle to Cape Town.

I spent the first couple of weeks or so in South Africa working at Southern Sun's President Hotel. Then I was bundled off to Plettenberg Bay, a beauty spot on the Garden Route, to shake up winter business at Southern Sun's Beacon Island Hotel. It was a magnificent 300 mile drive, albeit in an unreliable car I had had to buy in a rush. The hotel was stunning: a cantilevered building right on the beach with part of it jutting out to the sea and one of its restaurants actually underwater. It's since been converted into a timeshare-cum-hotel with fast food outlets in the once glorious lobby.

I stayed in the hotel initially but was then offered a cottage share with a couple from the hotel, Peter and Charlene, which I thought would make a nice change. The cottage was isolated and a car was necessary to get to the hotel and village. One evening, Charlene and I were alone in the cottage as Peter had gone to see his parents.

'I thought I might go to the hotel for a couple of hours,' said Charlene. 'Can I borrow your car?'

I willingly agreed as I'd decided to stay put for the evening.

Off she drove off and I went up to my bedroom.

A little while later, I heard a noise downstairs. I

presumed that it was Peter returning but when I called out to him, there was no reply.

'Peter?' I called again, and a scuffle ensued as the intruders rushed out of the house.

They had come through the kitchen window and the fridge door was wide open. They'd obviously come for food, but what might have followed when they realised there was a girl alone in a deserted cottage?

South Africa was (and still is) a dangerous place where rape and murder were commonplace. There was no telephone in the house, mobiles didn't exist, my car had gone and there were no occupied houses close by. It would have been dangerous to try and hoof it to the hotel; I was helpless and terrified and sat rigid with a poker in my hand until, mercifully, Peter returned. He took me to the hotel and I never went back to the cottage.

It emerged that when Charlene had heard noises outside, she decided to go to the hotel, *take my car* and say not a word. Unbelievable! The local Plettites were horrified by the story and thought I should carry a gun with me. Indeed, several were offered. I declined.

Plett was a pleasant place to spend a few months. I had a Christmas in the sun there and the totally delightful Gordon Mulholland, then a relatively unknown actor, came to entertain the guests and was wonderful company. At that time there was no television in South Africa, but it was soon to arrive and he became a household name in the country's favourite soap, *The Villagers*.

When my mission was accomplished workwise and the summer crowds would soon be arriving, I was dispatched 700 miles to Johannesburg to Southern Sun's head office. Somehow the ancient car made it but it was a hairy journey through countless thunderstorms.

There I found a flat in Hillbrow. At that time it was known as the Chelsea of Johannesburg, with some justification. There were plenty of trendy cafes and bijou shops, and it was quite a sought-after area if you didn't have the wherewithal for the smart northern suburbs. That was then. Today Hillbrow is riddled with crime, overcrowding, unemployment and poverty, and you visit the area at your peril. It's a sad reflection on the effects of post-apartheid South Africa – heartbreaking after the joy and hope for a country of peaceful co-existence when democratic South Africa finally came into being in 1994.

Hillbrow obviously wasn't *that* safe in my day either, as I was burgled twice during my relatively short time there. The first was on a Saturday. I'd been in the sitting room all afternoon and then went into the bedroom to change for an evening out. I opened the wardrobe doors and gazed into an empty space. All my clothes had gone! While I was in the sitting room, a quiet-footed person had come in, raided the wardrobe and departed. Nothing else was taken.

I wasn't on site for the second robbery. I returned to the flat after work, opened the door and was greeted by chaos. It had been ransacked; the contents of every drawer and cupboard thrown on the floor, even the bed stripped. As a virtual itinerant, I didn't have much of any value except for my jewellery. I had some nice pieces, particularly rings which had both real and sentimental value. I rushed to the stack of saucepans where my jewellery roll had been hidden – had the robbers found it? They had.

While waiting for the police to arrive, I picked up the bed linen strewn on the floor and there, underneath it, was my jewellery roll! A watch had been taken but everything else was there. It was a huge relief but why didn't they take it? It was small enough to be pushed into a pocket but instead they chose the watch and chucked the rest back. Fifty years later, I still have the same roll with its treasured contents, a home safe having replaced the saucepans. I can't remember what they did take – there couldn't have been many clothes – other than a pile of vinyl records, which I was sad about.

There didn't seem to be any proper job for me at Head Office so I became a roving ambassador for Southern Sun Hotels, travelling to their hotels all over South Africa to ensure their wheels were suitably oiled and hoping my wheels didn't give up the ghost. It couldn't have suited me better, as I was able to see a fair bit of this magnificent country and stay at their spectacular hotels. However, there wasn't enough work to keep me occupied so I was seamlessly transferred to Megan Carr Promotions, the go-to public relations company, courtesy of my Southern Sun boss and her friend, Megan. I was thirty-eight by now and life was still one big adventure.

PART TWO

CHAPTER 9

CAN YOU SEW?

by *Lindsay*

I was born and brought up at Harelaw, a farm in the Scottish Borders, not far north of Berwick-upon-Tweed. My mother's sister and freelance midwife, Auntie Pix, brought me into the world on 28 January 1952. There followed an idyllic childhood. Life was simple and my siblings and I – there were four of us, three girls and a boy – had free rein to roam. My parents, like so many of their generation who'd gone through boarding school and a war, were kind but slightly distant and undemonstrative. It wasn't until I was in my thirties that my father and I kissed on arrival and departure – at my instigation.

My primary school was in the nearby hamlet of Auchencrow, where the head (and only) teacher Mrs Elder ruled with a rod of iron or, more accurately, the tawse, the terrifying instrument of discipline that kept generations of Scottish children in line until as late as 1987. I escaped the long leather belt with its slit ends but other little girls and boys were not so lucky. On the plus side she was a superb teacher, as well as a firm believer in learning by rote and as a result I'm a splendid speller, completely reliable on times tables and can recite all the books of the Old and New Testament. In parallel, Mrs Elder was an enthusiastic champion of the arts, and we seemed to be always rehearsing for a concert or nativity play. Although tiny – there were only twenty or so pupils - Auchencrow Primary used to win cups the length and breadth of the Borders for Scottish country dancing, and I was a prize-winning speaker of verse in the vernacular.

While Mrs Elder's teaching spared me the fate of being sent away to school very young, my older sister Angela wasn't so fortunate. When the governess experiment didn't work out, she was shipped off to St Hilary's, fifty miles away in Edinburgh, aged eight. At least I was eleven when my turn came.

It wouldn't have been a surprise to encounter Miss Jean Brodie in her prime patrolling the corridors of St Hilary's. Like Sylvia's *alma mater*, Milton Mount College, nothing had changed since the war and indeed St Hilary's founder, Miss Muirhead, taught there for seven years in her salad days. It loosely followed the template of boys' boarding schools with prefects, house and nicknames – unsurprisingly I was, and still am, Swan. The food was predominantly starch based and, as a result, almost everyone went through a colossal and lumpy phase. Spots too, of course. My mother was fussy about how we looked but disappointingly for her it was some time before her maxim to 'Make the best of yourself' took hold. Simultaneously, she would invoke Nancy Mitford's 'No one's looking at you dear', when I was fretting about what to wear for teenage parties in my pudding years.

Our dorms still had blackout curtains, leftovers from the war. There was only rudimentary heating and on winter mornings we'd wake to a heavy frost on the inside of the windows. We were kept locked up for weeks on end, escaping only on one Saturday either side of half term.

St Hilary's girls were reared to be young ladies, suitable marriage material but not a lot else. Our matron, Miss Beth, dispensed malt and syrup of figs together with sage advice, which proved to be demonstrably untrue, such as 'Young ladies don't run in corridors' and the received wisdom in many girls' schools 'Sitting on hot pipes gives you piles.' Despite the thirteen years difference in our ages, there was no difference between Sylvia's Dickensian experience at Milton Mount and mine at St Hilary's.

Boys were rarely sighted, although we would peel off the crocodile on Sunday walks to meet the local bad lads. Afterwards, we'd return to the boarding house via the out-of-bounds sweetshop to stock up on penny chews and sherbet fountains, which we stuffed down our nylons.

The social highlight was the sixth form summer ball with one of the posh boys' schools that Scotland has in such profusion. They were seriously formal and we were assigned partners in advance, presumably to avoid the wallflower problem. Teacher patrols went into overdrive to flush out any snogging, of which there was plenty. Otherwise, we existed in a state of arrested development and, when we emerged into the waiting world at the end of the 1969 summer term, it was party time.

Towards the end of the fifth form, I woke one morning to the realisation that I was no longer willing to be a boarder. My mother took the news in good part and, with my aunt's help, arranged for me to lodge with Mr and Mrs Scott in Edinburgh's New Town. I loved this first taste of freedom and the Scotts proved delightful and unusual landlords, so much so that when my sister Angela married Andrew and they needed somewhere to live, their first home was a small flat chez Scott.

My university plans were initially thwarted when Maths O Level, which was required for admission to an arts degree, persistently eluded me. After four dismal attempts I had a spare year on my hands and, while languishing in the maths stream at Basil Paterson, Edinburgh's go-to crammer, I met someone whose Austrian friends urgently needed an au pair. I duly fetched up off the night train from Berwick via London and Calais in Wels, a town in Upper Austria, one January morning in 1970, a few days after my eighteenth birthday. My charming and kind host family, the von Potts, had two children when I arrived and three when I left six months later. They were part of the sprawling aristocracy left after the end of the Austro-Hungarian empire, the noble families of Austria. I travelled *en famille* to interesting places, met interesting people and stayed in extraordinarily grand places that had seen grander times. I was a reliable if ineffective childminder, but did well with housework and my German became fluent.

Halfway through I flew back home for a week's intensive maths tuition, the final roll of the dice, which stayed in my head just long enough for me to scrape through the damned exam. The doors of Edinburgh University swung open at last.

German and English Literature were my thing, and I left in 1973 with an MA. It was just as the Watergate scandal was brewing up badly for Richard Nixon and I vividly remember watching his resignation speech on the news. In 1974 the UK struggled under the infamous three-day week when the Conservative government and the trade unions were at each other's throats and the country was stricken by strikes.

The three-day week meant my job as a sales promotion

executive for medical publisher Churchill Livingstone didn't impinge on the rest of my life. Which was fortunate, as it was relentlessly dull. Medical publishing soon gave way to dictionaries when, despite having none of the necessary skills or experience, I was offered the job of Publicity Editor for W&R Chambers, publisher of the famous Chambers Twentieth Century Dictionary. It came with a secretary, a large office in the New Town and a spot in the underground car park. I loved it even though I wasn't to be there for long.

In my second year at university, I became engaged to the sweetest man who was universally adored by my whole family, dogs included. So much so that when the initial sugar rush abated, I found myself in a bit of a bind as the direction of travel was definitely up the aisle. Decent job, delightful fiancé, what more could I want? Answer: see the world, taste adventure, live. My family was displeased. *Tant pis*.

Goodbye Scotland, hello South Africa. All change.

Mary, my schoolfriend-turned-Edinburgh flatmate, and I set sail from Southampton for Cape Town aboard the RMS Pendennis Castle on 18 July 1975. I'd returned my engagement ring, Mary had extracted herself from her latest love affair and we were ready for the world, or at least South Africa. A pocket Venus since our early teens, blonde and vivacious Mary always had a succession of beaux lining up outside our flat in Edinburgh, and inevitably I was the one who had to deal with their broken hearts. She was the perfect companion for my big adventure.

We struck out from Cape Town for Johannesburg on the twenty-five-hour train journey across the semi desert of the Karoo, arriving early one Saturday morning. For the first few days we stayed in the Chelsea Hotel in Hillbrow:

super hip then; no man's land now.

Mary's frightfully well-connected Edinburgh wine merchant boss had fixed up a job for her and she started work almost at once, but when I turned up to take up the post of management trainee I'd been offered before leaving Scotland, I was greeted with blank faces and directed to a company in Johannesburg's smart Northern Suburbs, known to be on the lookout for promotions girls - not that I realised I was one.

My diary for 13 August 1975 records that I met Sylvia Holder at 11.45 a.m. precisely.

'You must be the new girl. Can you sew?' were her first words.

I was actually there to be interviewed as a supermarket promotions girl for Tic Tacs, those little mints that taste nice for the first few seconds and then, in my case at least, get spat out. The link between sewing and Tic Tacs wasn't immediately obvious and I hesitantly offered, 'Well, yes, a bit.'

That was the extent of my interview at Megan Carr Promotions, or MCP, Johannesburg's most effortlessly glamorous all-female PR company. Things like a CV, references and so on seemed superfluous. Even questions. I assumed that was how they did things in *South Efrica* then.

I seemed to be what Sylvia was looking for. She handed me a needle and thread and set me to sewing a banner for the launch of the South African chapter of *The Wombles*, the pointy-nosed, litter-picking band of Great Uncle Bulgaria and his furry sidekicks, of which more later.

It was a 'sliding doors' moment: the mix-up changed my life forever.

And Sylvia's.

I never did find out what happened to the real new girl.

My boss was tall, slim and blue-jeaned with an air of total confidence. 'Fearless' is the right word for Sylvia. I'd never met anyone like her before and I haven't since.

Thus began an adventure which took us both from mid 1970s Johannesburg to running our eponymous PR company in London's Camden Town. Almost fifty years later, we're still the very best of friends.

MCP's office was in Sandton Office Tower, the newly built jewel in Joburg's commercial crown. Apart from the rather hideous 270m-high JG Strijdom Tower, it was the highest building for miles around and soared above the newly opened Sandton City shopping mall. From the fifteenth floor we looked out across the Olympic-sized swimming pools and bougainvillea-filled gardens of the prosperous Northern suburbs and beyond to the township of Alexandra, where the *nie-blankes,* the non-whites, as black and mixed-race Africans were labelled, lived. If ever there was a contrast between the haves and have-nots, it was exemplified from the fifteenth floor of the Sandton Tower.

If I close my eyes, I can see the MCP office that first day in August 1975 as I hovered in reception, waiting to be transformed into a Tic Tac girl. The whole floor was divided by white partitions into mini offices, onto each of which was fixed a ceramic bird painted with the name of the occupant. On the other side of the partitions sat the lovely daughters of some of Johannesburg's oldest and wealthiest families: blonde, lightly tanned, exquisitely dressed and equipped with insouciance and self-confidence. Sally Ann was cool, green-eyed and beautiful, while Trisha's blonde curls bounced in a Tiggerish way, matching her approach to life. They came from that magic circle of the super-rich and well connected, which meant they were the best of friends. The whole gorgeousness was presided over by the charismatic Megan Carr, South Africa's hottest divorcée.

Each morning the Golden Girls would emerge from their gleaming BMWs and Mercedes looking divine – 'divine' was the word; everything was divine in the lives of the gilded youth of 1975 South Africa. Life was a combination of work doing something stylish; an enormous, stunning and fully staffed home *chez les parents*; holidays in Europe and weekends in a holiday house on the Cape or the Vaal River. The expression 'another world' doesn't even begin to describe the difference between the one I'd left behind in grey 1970s Scotland, or more particularly, the huge contrast to lives being lived just a few miles away from Sandton City in the townships of Soweto and Alexandra.

Sylvia hadn't been in town long, having come from working in the Cape, the most recent stop in her globe-trotting life. A couple of years in South Africa cured her travel bug and it was London from then on.

MCP's client list was varied. There were rather routine instore promotions of the Tic Tac type and more general PR events which called on the high-octane glamour of the Golden Girls. Anyone who needed the oxygen of publicity in Johannesburg and beyond called up Megan Carr.

When Elizabeth Beresford, creator of TV characters and environmental enthusiasts, *The Wombles*, arrived off the mail ship in 1975 to unleash her furry creations on South Africa, she too headed straight for MCP.

By the time I found my way to the fifteenth floor of Sandton Tower, Sylvia was masterminding the launch. She'd relocated the Wombles from the green and pleasant suburban safety of London's Wimbledon Common to the parched mine dumps of the Witwatersrand, a bold decision given that at that time at least, Joburg often seemed to tremble with subterranean collapses in the old gold mines. At any moment the Wombles could have been swallowed up. Perish the thought. Perish the Wombles.

My first few weeks passed in a flurry of fake fur as we rushed all over town in Sylvia's ancient *caffè latte* two-toned Morris 1100 – not for her the Mercs and Beemers – delivering the Wombles' clean-up message to the waiting world. I was in the 'skin', as the costumes were unappealingly known, or a succession of skins; Sylvia was keeping the show on the road and stoking Womble fever. My day's work could range from a personal appearance as Great Uncle Bulgaria at a supermarket opening and autograph signing at a school or drive-in cinema, to a photocall as Madame Cholet in a skip. For proper paid-for bookings, of which there were surprisingly many, I was generally a reserve Womble as a cheerful group of Witwatersrand University students had first dibs. For bigger gigs, we'd travel all around the towns on the Highveld in a battered VW van driven by Hitler, the MCP driver.

CHAPTER 10

THE BURTONS COME TO TOWN

by Lindsay

Just as I was settling into my 'skin', hot on the Wombles' heels came a completely different kettle of fish. Well, more a can of worms.

In the 1970s, Celebrity Tennis was just getting off the ground. A few tournaments had been successful in the States and, as well as raising money for charity, they provided a way for stars who might be starting to lose their sparkle to step back into the spotlight and travel the world.

For reasons that have never been clear, MCP picked up the Celebrity Tennis baton – or racquet. Not long after I'd taken up my position in Sylvia's office, word came that the first ever South African Celebrity Tennis tournament was coming to town and our task was to whip up a frenzy of excitement and sell a stadium of tickets.

Celebrity Tennis involved tennis, although not of the kind that people pay good money to watch. But the chance to see some serious Hollywood glitz was irresistible. At least, that was the plan.

Things stalled initially when the list of the stars was revealed in a series of calls with the Hollywood agent. Poised to board the SA bound jet were Rod Steiger, Jill St John, Dyan Cannon, Dino Martin, Dean Martin's handsome son, The Three Degrees, John Marley, Micky Dolenz and Davy

Jones of The Monkees, Ringo Starr and Peter Lawford. It's fair to say some of the names didn't send pulses racing, apart from The Monkees, Ringo and The Three Degrees – apparently the then Prince Charles was a big fan. This was pre-Google and, despatched by Sylvia to the library reference section, I could find nothing that gave us any confidence that these celebs might be enough to fill the cavernous space of Ellis Park, home to South African rugby. Everyone was beginning to have cold feet and it looked as though Celebrity Tennis would be cancelled. However, with just over a month to go, we were winding down to the weekend when Megan made an announcement.

'We've got Burton and Taylor!'

Word had come from Hollywood that the two biggest stars in the firmament, the planet's most newsworthy couple would be heading south. Elizabeth Taylor and Richard Burton, albeit in between marriages to each other at the time, were on their way to Joeys.

Everything changed in that instant. The smelly fake fur was put into storage as the Wombles gave way to Celebrity Tennis. Back on the fifteenth floor of Sandton City it was all hands to the pump. Tickets needed to be sold, PR needed to be done, stars needed to be entertained.

There's nothing simple about dealing with divas and Elizabeth Taylor was the biggest diva of them all. There was the entourage: Gavin de Becker, her young assistant, who went on to found America's most prestigious private security firm; her hairdresser, and Richard's personal maid, Madame Glaz, plus tons of luggage. And then there was the dog. Elizabeth didn't travel without it and international animal export rules meant nothing to her. No dog? No tennis. The dog was a deal-breaker and so contacts were leveraged, as we would say today, and we became fixated on the dog.

And then suddenly things moved on, as if the dog had never been and the Taylor/Burton security became the preoccupation du jour.

The personal security business was in its infancy in 1975 Joburg, but the imminent approach of the gods of stage and screen required swift and decisive action. Happily, among the MCP network was someone with contacts in the bodyguard fraternity. I hesitate to suggest it was the Johannesburg underworld, we didn't delve too closely, but the outcome was an introduction to Chen Sam. Taken on as a bodyguard, Chen Sam was to become Elizabeth's publicist for life. In 1993, she went on record in the *Chicago Tribune* to reveal that they'd met in 1972 when the Burtons were in Botswana and South Africa to promote black tennis and black theatre. She recalled how Richard had contracted malaria and she'd drawn on her doctorate in pharmacology for tropical diseases to treat him. Given they hadn't been even introduced until 1975 this came as a surprise to us, as did the doctorate. Her recollection was not Sylvia's and mine – *and we were there*. But all credit to Chen for seizing the moment and the narrative. She and Elizabeth stayed friends for life, which wasn't what could be said of Elizabeth's exes.

When the Burton Taylors swept into town a few weeks later in a triumphant Trump-style motorcade, the burghers of Johannesburg lined the streets to witness Hollywood hitting the Highveld. From the motorcade Sylvia waved to the cheering crowds, channelling the Queen Mum to a tee.

'There was something strange about seeing these huge global stars in 3D as they came off the plane,' Sylvia told me afterwards. Big stars aren't usually big people and they looked somehow much smaller that she'd expected, even though a fair number of celebs had already crossed her path in her earlier incarnations.

Of course, Elizabeth and Richard had no intention of lifting a racquet, but they shook things up in sleepy Joburg. The whiff of an engagement in the air sent the diamond dealers checking their safes for the best and biggest rocks.

After a few celebrity tantrums of varying intensity, we all fetched up at Ellis Park Stadium Johannesburg, beloved of rugby fans the world over, on Friday 26 September 1975.

On this day Ellis Park was filled not with raucous rugby supporters but by what would kindly be described as an enthusiastic crowd. They'd come to unlovely downtown Joburg today not to witness Grand Slam tennis but to see royalty close up.

Hollywood royalty.

In the super VIP seats at Ellis Park, the President of South Africa's arrival was imminent and although protocol demanded he must be the last to take his seat, Elizabeth and Richard weren't there. No trace. Word came that, never a martyr to punctuality, Elizabeth was in the bath. And Richard? Another heavy night, perhaps.

Under the chatter of the expectant crowds, I became aware of a testy conversation being conducted on a short-range radio. In Sylvia's clear and perfectly enunciated tones the message was passed:

'Tell Elizabeth to get out of the effing bath. Now.'

Meanwhile, the South African president, Dr Nicolaas Diederichs, and his wife had already emerged from the presidential limo and it fell to my unlucky lot to entertain them in the Ellis Park cafeteria, a place of great simplicity with a limited range of refreshments. Presidents usually receive the red carpet and reception committee. Why they were presented with me as a twenty-three-year-old newbie, I don't know. Where was Megan Carr?

It seemed odd then. It seems odd now. I'm sure they found it odd too.

The intervening time, while we awaited the arrival of La Taylor, seemed to stretch into hours and conversation flagged.

'Do you have grandchildren, Dr Diederichs?'

'Is the garden at Presidential House pretty at this time of year?'

'Do you play tennis?'

My predicament was not helped by the president's first language being Afrikaans, and my limited repertoire of small talk was quickly exhausted. Things hadn't started particularly well when I'd had to blag some cash – not from him – to provide hospitality in the form of two coffees. Why didn't I stick with being a Tic Tac girl? I didn't sign up for coffee with the President of South Africa.

With hindsight, a livelier but riskier topic of conversation might have been about his Swiss bank account.

'How are your 28 million rand doing in Switzerland, Mr President?' would have put the cat well and truly among the pigeons.

I found out later that while acting as Minister of Finance, Dr Diederichs had agreed to transfer South Africa's gold from London to Zurich and en route had squirrelled away a few grams for himself – quite a few, apparently – in a Swiss bank account. Robert Smit, a former SA representative on the IMF, was murdered after telling a colleague that he was about to expose a massive scandal about a Swiss bank. The finger of suspicion pointed at Dr D, or Dr Gold as he came to be known, but that was two years after our encounter in that rather unexciting café.

Elizabeth eventually got out of the bath and made a grand entrance with Richard in a haze of hairspray and vodka. I remember her being dressed, a little unexpectedly, in a navy-blue T-shirt decorated with the Coca Cola logo in Hebrew, headscarf, large gold hoop earrings and a tight pair of jeans. The talk was that she'd lost weight on a trip to Israel a few weeks before – hence the tight jeans.

In the VIP box Sylvia was busy getting things organised. 'If you would sit here, please, Elizabeth, and you here, Richard, the president will sit between you and his wife will sit on your other side, Richard.'

'No,' said Richard. 'I will sit next to Elizabeth.'

Sylvia tried again. 'We would be grateful as the protocol would be awkward if they were not to sit with you.'

'I do not wish to sit next to the president. I wish to sit next to my wife [she wasn't at the time], and that is what I will do.'

Sylvia's patience was by now sorely tested. 'Do please sit where you like until they arrive, and then you might like to sit next to the president,' she persevered.

But they didn't.

Sylvia marked them down as rude and spoilt, and they gave us no reason to revise her opinion over the coming weeks.

Time hung heavy as the lack of any tennis-playing skills in the visiting celebs was a barrier to a programme of decent games. The tournament MC was Sir Henry Grattan-Bellew, a well-known South African sports commentator of Irish extraction, who did his best to hold things together but at one point had a really ghastly tantrum. The raw material of celebs with negligible tennis skills, a few valiant local players, a herd of Wombles (hastily assembled to fill in the gaps), and a band of minstrels who rejoiced in the extraordinarily un-PC name of the Coon Carnival, was too much, even for a seasoned pro like Sir H. The final straw was the no show of the *Ipi Tombi* musical stars, delayed by some horrific traffic pile-up and the realisation that the Wombles would have to return to the court and womble on.

Once again, I found myself in a position for which I was uniquely unsuited and unqualified, this time as the commentator at SA Celebrity Tennis.

'Ladies and gentlemen, boys and girls, I am thrilled to give you once again the latest global sensation: The Wombles!'

Applause was restrained and it was a relief when Sir Henry was wheedled back behind the microphone by one of the Golden Girls.

Celebrity Tennis culminated in a celebrity banquet. On the night of 28 September 1975, the great, the good and the very definitely not-so-good of Johannesburg donned their rocks and frocks and took the limo to the Carlton Hotel in Main Street for the 'A Night with the Stars' celebrity banquet.

The Carlton was South Africa's most famous hotel. Mick Jagger, Whitney Houston, Margaret Thatcher and Hillary Clinton all stayed there in its heyday, and Nelson Mandela celebrated his seventy-fifth birthday in the very same ballroom where the celebrity banquet had happened eighteen years earlier. By the nineties its glory days were behind it and the Carlton closed in 1998. Our celebs stayed at the newly opened Landdrost in Plein Street, which I suppose offered a better deal. It's closed now, too. Another monument to a very different time.

Things had started to go off-script in the morning of the banquet when a row broke out over where the reigning Miss World, Anneline Kriel, should sit. She was actually the runner-up but had claimed the crown when UK's Helen Morgan was found to be an unmarried mother and had to step down. Extraordinary to think of that happening nowadays.

'Anneline will sit next to Richard,' her boyfriend told Sylvia.

'I'm sorry, but she can't. The seating's for Celebrity Tennis stars only. It's just not possible, there are no spaces at the top table.'

At the point where dust was starting to fly and handbags were being reached for, Sylvia decided this wasn't a battle worth fighting.

'Sit where you like,' she told them (I'm not sure if the eff word was in play but the sentiment was) and stepped away for things to take their course.

And they did.

It was all getting a bit much for me and rather strangely (with hindsight) I headed for the suite where the delightful and cheerful Three Degrees were based, and they settled me down with everyday girl chat. Ever since then when I reach the point of combustion over some perceived bad behaviour, which in my defence is infrequent, Sylvia and I describe it as a 'Three Degrees'.

The evening progressed pleasantly enough after that with a robust performance of 'When Will I See You Again?' belted out by The Three Degrees. There may have been something from The Monkees, even Ringo; I don't recall. There was an auction which included some Taylor Burton items, prompting a frenzy of bids.

But things took a major nosedive at some point around the pudding course. Word came from the Taylor Burton *laager* that Elizabeth wouldn't be flying on the private plane laid on for the celebs to progress on safari to Botswana, Rhodesia (as it then was) and Kruger National Park the following day. Being private wasn't enough; it had to be a private *jet*.

Mike Todd, the third of Elizabeth's seven husbands and the only one she didn't divorce, had been killed in a propeller plane crash and from then on it was jets all the way. Basic telephones barely functioned in South Africa back in those days and finding a private jet is tricky at the best of times but late on a Sunday evening when drink had been taken, it could have been beyond the possible. Happily, the Golden Girls moved in the right circles and a jet appeared, as if from nowhere.

With Elizabeth's entourage of assistant and personal maid plus the many suitcases onboard, there was no room for the other stars who had to fly by propellor plane to Victoria Falls, led of course by Sylvia, before being decanted onto an ancient bus for the eighty-mile journey along bush roads to Chobe Lodge. Spirits slumped when the bus broke down en route but were lifted by an impromptu performance by Micky Dolenz and Davy Jones.

Meanwhile, having arrived before everyone else in their own private jet at Chobe, Elizabeth and Richard, by now in full courtship mode, lost no time in inflicting their own particular brand of demanding behaviour on everyone. It may have been the depths of the African bush but for Elizabeth her appearance was still the number one priority. Back in Sandton City I was parrying press calls on rumours that the Taylor Burtons had been lost. Thanks to Telex I was able to reach Sylvia, deep in the African bush, who by now had had more than she could stand of bad diva behaviour and sent back the one liner for my eyes only:

Confirm the Burtons are missing

Wishful thinking on her part.

Having caused a near diplomatic incident by refusing to go to Rhodesia, where huge and complicated arrangements had been made to host their visit, Richard and Elizabeth turned up just over a fortnight later beside the Chobe River on 10 October 1975 for their second wedding, performed by the local district commissioner and witnessed by two Chobe employees. Richard snapped up a colossal diamond ring from a Joburg jeweller on his way back from Chobe.

Diamonds may be forever and love lovelier the second time around, but not in this case. They divorced, again, the following year.

CHAPTER 11
AND THE CIRCUS MOVED ON

by Lindsay

Everything felt rather flat after the A and B-listers returned to Tinseltown. It was back into the Womble suits for me, but Sylvia decided to chance her arm by going freelance. As PR was in its infancy in South Africa, she found herself earning good money. But then, in true Sylvia style, she chucked it all in and sailed from Durban for Southampton on the SA Vaal in December 1975. She could no longer stand living in a country whose people were segregated according to the colour of their skin.

I'd met Richard, who later became my husband, at the captain's cocktail party on the Pendennis Castle. Approaching, glass in hand, he'd invited me to dance but I'd very ungraciously – and inaccurately - replied, 'I'm not accustomed to dancing with drunks,' and so that was that until he turned up later at the community house where Mary and I lived in Johannesburg's northern suburbs. Things progressed and we spent our weekends travelling to places like Swaziland (now Eswatini) and Lesotho in his huge old 1960s Chrysler, which he called Al Capone. One weekend we flew in a five-seater plane piloted by Rudy, a Swiss part-time pilot, and camped in the open air on an island in the Okavango Delta in Botswana before flying low over Victoria Falls. The plane was a little ropy and at one point the door flew open at take-off and Richard was almost sucked out. All part of the adventure.

After Celebrity Tennis, which didn't turn the profit it had been expected to, there were many bills to be paid. The MCP office moved from the fifteenth floor with its striking view to more modest quarters further down the building, which Megan also leased. Life became infinitely less exciting. Apart from the Wombles, my daily diet became more packet curry than Carlton Hotel banquet as a new client needed in-store cooking demos for a new curry product set up in supermarkets all over Gauteng province. I had to galvanise cooks in Pretoria, Benoni, Brakpan and other rather unlovely towns around Johannesburg. It wasn't quite the same.

More importantly, June 1976 was the time of the Soweto Uprising, which spread across the townships. From Sandton City we could see Alexandra Township burning. One autumn day the MCP accountant, another Sylvia, called us to reception, took a gun out of her handbag and put it on the desk. It was for us to use if there was any trouble. The time had come for me to go.

Richard and I flew to Blantyre in Malawi, hung out round the lake and then travelled up through much of East Africa, stopping in Tanzania and Kenya for our first ever safari and back via Egypt to the UK. In Cairo, although hotels were full with people who'd fled the civil war in Lebanon and there was hardly a room to be had, further up the Nile there was hardly a tourist to be seen and we were the only living things in the Valley of the Kings, apart from a few edgy dogs. Not many people can claim to have seen Tutankhamun's tomb alone but we did. We were almost the only people in the Temple of Karnak too.

Back from our travels, Richard went to work in Holland, where he'd had a job after university and before his busman's holiday in South Africa. I became assistant editor of a new business magazine, despite having none of the relevant experience. It didn't seem to matter. The people I met then are friends still and *Company Secretary's Review*, now online, has prospered. Weekends were spent flying between London and Amsterdam until we got married and rented a little flat on the Amstel Kanaal. Amsterdam was heavenly; the only snag was finding a job. However, those were the anorexic years and I signed up with Euromodels, a smart agency with headquarters on the exclusive Herengracht, and did a few seasons for the Dutch agents of a German clothing company, who chose me because they liked speaking English. I wasn't Cindy Crawford by even the greatest stretch of the imagination, but my employers were delightful and it was great fun. I was able to earn decent amounts of money. It was enough to pay the deposit on our first house back in London.

In the early eighties Richard worked during the week in Paris, where he shared a flat with Bjørn, a sweet-natured Norwegian engineer, in the Boulevard Richard Lenoir, not far from the Bastille. Parisian weekends became routine and friends often came along for the ride, including Mary and her by now husband, Peter. Over dinner one evening in the Art Nouveau surroundings of Julien in the Rue du Faubourg Saint Denis, we were startled when a familiar-looking diner at the next table, leant over.

'Sounds like you're speaking English.'

Turning to where the voice came from, we did a double take. We were only sitting next to the Rolling Stones' Keith Richards and Ronnie Wood. They were in

Paris to record the *Undercover* album and Ronnie and his girlfriend Jo were in high spirits as she'd just found out she was pregnant. We celebrated with champagne and by the time we left, the restaurant was empty and the waiters openly yawning. Ronnie was a delight, explaining that Mick Jagger wasn't there as Jerry Hall had just arrived in town, which meant they could go out without being bothered by fans. Forty years on, he and Keith look much the same now as they did then. Once a rock star, always a rock star.

CHAPTER 12
FIRST DAYS OF THE EMPIRE

by Sylvia

I have much to thank the late Sir David Lindsay Keir for, one time Master of Balliol College, Oxford. Unwittingly, from beyond the grave, he was responsible for the setting up of Holder Swan Public Relations, which Lindsay and I ran for more than twenty-three years through ups and downs, triumphs (mostly) and disasters (few). They were happy and hectic years, but would never have happened had it not been for Sir David.

Lindsay had returned to the UK sometime after me and spent a year in Amsterdam with Richard, by now her husband. I'd asked her if she could help out for a couple of days at Biggs Holder Associates, the PR company I'd set up with Suzie Biggs, whom I knew from my Carlton Tower days when she was the PR at Grosvenor House. We'd got together for a drink one evening and over a haze of alcohol decided to set up our own company, a small fish in the vast London pond of PR companies. Our working styles were very different and it was not ideal to hear on our first day of operation that she was pregnant, but we rubbed along well enough. Now we were in need of some extra help over a busy period.

Lindsay was happy to come in for a few days and it was wonderful working with her again. The days soon stretched to weeks. Sadly, there was no prospect of our being able to offer her anything full time and, inevitably, the time came when she went in search of a proper PR job, not least perhaps because of her working conditions with us, which wouldn't have met the legal requirement – a card table in a leaking passage! Unsurprisingly, she was immediately offered an account executive position with Lexington, the PR wing of the mega advertising agency J Walter Thompson, with a big desk in her own office.

It just required the nod from the chairman and Lindsay duly turned up for her confirmation interview. She thought it was going rather well and the deal was all but signed when the chairman, who'd been studying her CV, randomly asked, 'Are you related to David Lindsay Keir?' She shares two of his names.

Thinking this was a feather in her cap, Lindsay duly explained he was her granny's cousin after whom she was named – her parents had been hoping for a boy at the time. Alas, the chairman wasn't a fan. As Master of Balliol, 'Uncle David' had denied him an undergraduate place there. The interview ended abruptly and the rejection letter arrived the next day.

'Hurrah, let's crack open the champagne,' I thought but did not say.

I commiserated of course, but selfishly was secretly delighted that there'd been a reprieve although I knew she'd soon find another good job.

Serendipity was waiting in the wings. Unexpectedly, Suzie decided to become a full-time mother and was away to her cradle duties. Lindsay was on board. We set up a new company, Holder Swan Public Relations. From the very start, with no hint of irony, the new company was known as the Empire aka the Emp, the name even adopted by some of our clients.

I was thrilled at this unexpected turn of events. Lindsay and I had a lot of fun working together in South Africa and now we were going to be partners of our own PR company in London. We'd become firm friends, a friendship which is of huge importance to us both and has flourished over nearly fifty years. Lindsay is extraordinary – a one-off, clever, funny, very silly and fiercely loyal friend. You could never be bored in her company. Our quirky sense of humour delights us both, as does our own vocabulary, built up over the years, which leaves others mystified.

The rules were drawn up: No dreary clients and win or lose an account, we'd crack open a bottle of champagne. *Absolutely Fabulous* mirrored us some years later in a more upmarket style – theirs was 'Bolly' while ours came from the local discount store. We stuck to the fizz principle but did find ourselves reduced to taking on one or two dreary clients in the direst of recessions. Advertising and PR always bear the brunt of companies' economies.

We needed an office large enough to be able to sublet some rooms and thus, hopefully, live rent free. Our first was the whole of the top floor of the three-building Post Office in Parkway, in the heart of Camden Town where the streets converge. After a lick of paint and a new carpet, we had three rooms to let, which brought in the cash to pay for our rent. We acquired a large partners' desk and sat opposite each other for the next twenty-three years and Lindsay acquired Jessie, a Jack Russell Terrier, who accompanied her to work every day and became known as our Chairdog.

Business partnerships with friends can so often end in tears but we never fell out. Critically, we were not competitive with each other and shared the same ethos of hard work and professionalism, but always found time for laughter and silliness. We still do. We certainly didn't come out of the normal PR stable but clients liked our *modus operandi* – telling things as they were and not making false promises – even if some thought us a little strange. We were rather conspicuous, both of us being very tall, and one client said we reminded him of the comedy duo Hinge and Bracket. We happily adopted the voices of Dr Evadne and Dame Hilda on demand.

PART ONE

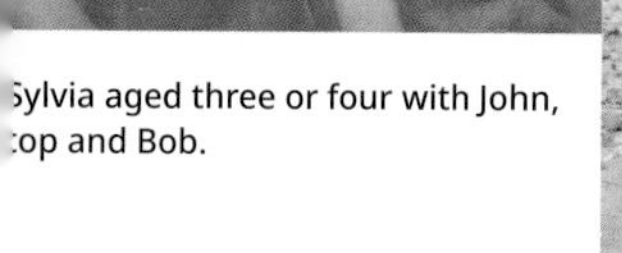

Sylvia aged three or four with John, top and Bob.

The Holder family on holiday at Birchington on Sea, obviously during rationing and when ties were worn on the beach.

Milton Mount College, Sylvia's school. It looks grand but was already in a bad state of repair when she was there. The house was later demolished to make way for a huge block of flats but the Round Pond and the beautiful gardens survive.

Sylvia's important announcement.

Avon Castle in Ringwood. Bought by Sylvia's mama for £16,500 in 1961.

The ensemble hasn't quite the caché of the original Cecil Beaton creation for Audrey Hepburn in *My Fair Lady*. Sylvia's effort, in swathes of flowered paper used for Andrex loo rolls, proved a good publicity stunt.

Sylvia's parents, circa 1966, during their hap
stay in New Mexico. They would have been i
their early sixties.

Sylvia and Margaret left, propping up the bar.

Sylvia in Hong Kong with Fred, her beloved TR3. There were even queues on the Clearwater Bay Road in 1970.

ylvia's sybaritic Hong Kong lifestyle. The
hampagne must have just been out of
hot.

Thirty years on. Sylvia enjoying a lunch in Sausalito with Brenda during their nostalgic return to San Francisco.

PART TWO

Lindsay, left and sister Angela in the garden at Harelaw.

Fancy dress aboard the RMS Pendennis Castle. Lindsay with Mary en route to Cape Town.

Sylvia, left and the cream of Johannesburg's police force greet Elizabeth Taylor and Richard Burton.

Lindsay did a few seasons for Euromodels in Amsterdam.

Holder Swan's office at 70 Chalk Farm Road, said to be the original Chalk Farm farmhouse and artist Walter Sickert's studio.

Lindsay with Richard, Ben and baby Georgina.

A Zambia press trip. Nice work if you can get it!

Lindsay outside the Fleet Sandwich Bar with the Coreen Munt Agency above.

On the steps at 70 Chalk Farm Road for the FT feature on our 'How To Do Your Own PR' seminars.

Credit Alan Harper/*Financial Times* © Financial Times Limited.

Sylvia surrounded by some of the Chichester Festival Theatre stars – and SuperTed.

Lindsay with 007 himself. Roger Moore was one of Charles de Temple's celebrity guests.

Sylvia in the swag-lined press tent at our first Hampton Court Palace International Flower Show.

With Jessie the Chairdog.

PART THREE

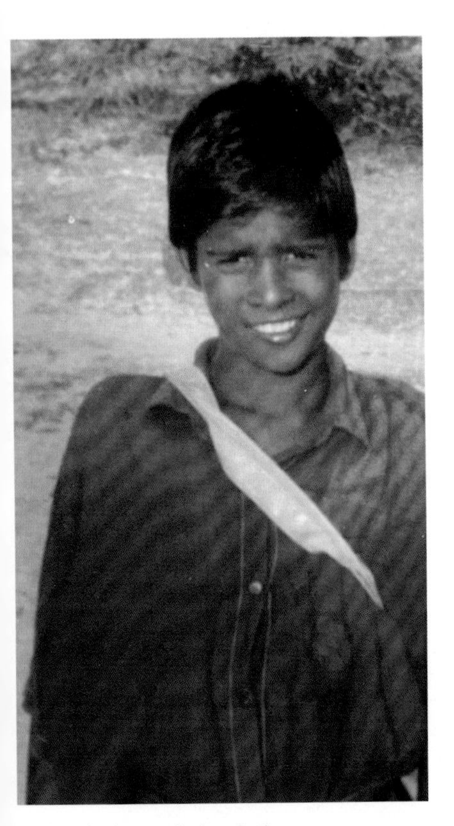

Venkat, the boy on the beach, the day Sylvia met him.

All along the beach, the colourful boats line up ready for the night's fishing.

Sylvia and JR in the boatyard on the beach set up by the Venkat Trust's Kovalam Tsunami Appeal to build catamarans to replace fishing boats lost in the disaster.

Sylvia and JR having a smashing time before PUPS rebuilding gets underway.

Many of Kovalam's houses were in a desperate state.

JR served for two terms as President of Kovalam.

A warm PUPS welcome.

The Trust's makeover of PUPS successfully turned it into a happy and productive school.

PUPS is a school buzzing with happy, motivated children.

Credit John Sargent

Pupils mark out the site of the High School but it took three frustrating years for it to be built.

The thousand pupils line up outside Kovalam Higher Secondary School, a place of academic and sporting excellence.

At last, the High School is officially open. Sylvia and JR cut the ribbon with a local Tamil Nadu dignatory.

The JR Hall was bursting at the seams on the official opening day.

Thanks to the language lab, both written and spoken English have improved beyond recognition.

Gardening lessons in the Gwyneth Powell Memorial Garden on the roof of the Higher Secondary School.

Udayakumar cut out a photo of himself and added it to his sponsor family's picture.

Trustee John and Sylvia with her British Empire Medal 'for services to education in Kovalam, India'.

JR and Ali's families, from left Ali, Abebabi, Nafila, Sumaya, Balaji, JR, Uma and Thanuja.

As well as keeping on top of all the children's academic performances and being a listening ear for any problems they may have, Aarthi is super creative.

The Lakshmi House palm tree and papaya are watered by the monsoon.

Sylvia travels around Kovalam in the TukTuk she gave herself for her 80th birthday.

Happy Birthday Sylvia Mam. The Big Birthday Bash guests.

Sylvia and her boys. With JR and Ali cutting her 80th birthday cake.

Dear Venkat, you did not die in vain.

CHAPTER 13

HIGH FLYERS

by Lindsay

Although we walked the PR walk in our shoulder pads and stilettos, we didn't talk the PR talk. We weren't like other London PR women in the late seventies and early eighties, insofar as we weren't – and aren't – smooth talkers. PRs are generally expected to sweet-talk journalists and clients but we told it like it was. The Emp was a flannel-free zone, which didn't work for everyone. But if clients liked us, they really liked us and ditto the press.

There was a dress code in those days. Jeans, T shirts and flip flops weren't an option and we enjoyed dressing up. Sylvia was a regular at the Harvey Nicks and Harrods sales, and we both tapped into the most marvellous seam of beautiful clothes via Sylvia's friend Anna, who worked at Anglia Television when she returned from Canada with the well-known producer, Brenda Reid. Brenda was the same size as us both and a serious clothes shopper. Every so often she would have a wardrobe clear-out and a treasure trove of hardly, if ever, worn designer clothes and accessories would arrive in black bin bags. I had some of Brenda's beautiful suits and jackets until not long ago when the moths took them.

In my early days as a temp at the Emp, Sylvia and Suzie's hotel backgrounds meant there were quite a few hotel and restaurant clients. After Suzie moved on and I took my place at the partners' desk, we used our Africa experience to broaden our horizons.

So began the Zambia years. Until then, most clients had come through word of mouth but in early 1980, a recession arrived and PR became a disposable luxury for many companies, thus forcing us to turn to energetic self-promotion. We wrote lots of 'cold call' letters to the kind of companies we would like to work for, more in hope than expectation, and were thrilled when invited to attend the offices of Zambia Airways in London smart St James's to meet Mr Mulenga (not his real name), the London boss.

The interview bore more than a passing resemblance to mine with Sylvia in South Africa five years previously. Mr Mulenga seemed unconcerned about what we would do or how we would do it.There was no presentation, no competition, no fretting about how we performed in the interview, what we might or might not have said better – just a friendly chat, followed by a friendly handshake and Zambia Airways, which we referred to thereafter by its QZ call sign[4] joined the Emp's client list.

'When can you start?' asked Mr Mulenga.

'Now,' we answered in chorus.

Afterwards, I remember Sylvia doing a scissor jump with delight as we swept past the Ritz. Then common sense prevailed and we turned sharp left for a suitably glitzy Ritzy celebration.[5]

We were beside ourselves with joy at our new client but at the time didn't realise the extent of the joy that was

4 Taken over as Indonesia AirAsia's call sign after Zambia Airways' demise.

5 Some years later Sylvia received an urgent telephone call from Mr Mulenga, by then languishing in Lusaka jail. We weren't able to establish why or how we could help, but it reminded us that things aren't always as they might seem.

to come and the serious job that was to be done. By the 1980s, the 250,000 elephants that had once roamed Zambia's savannahs had been reduced through poaching to the low thousands. Zambia needed the foreign exchange western tourism could deliver and, equally importantly, for the world to wake up to the looming environmental catastrophe.

Our job was to introduce its wonders to the safari market – individuals and prospective tour operators – through the press. In those days, long before social media and the dilution of the importance of print, a national press travel feature had the power to drive extraordinary levels of bookings. A piece in the weekend travel pages of the right newspaper would bring in hundreds if not thousands of enquiries when offices opened the following Monday.

It took a bit of juggling on my part as I'd become a mother by now. Ben arrived in 1985, eight years after Richard and I were married, and Georgy was born in 1987, and so fitting in work wasn't straightforward, far less travelling to Africa. Richard's job took him here, there and everywhere during the week, and the nanny was a vital member of the household. Some nannies were wonderful, others were not and the same was true of au pairs in the later years. We managed, but in 1995 I wasn't sad to say goodbye to our last ever au pair: Guy, a twenty-one-year-old American student. Ben was sorry to see him go. He'd taught him all kinds of life skills, including how to hop over underground ticket gates to dodge the fare and chat up girls.

It wasn't difficult to enlist the travel journalists' A-list. There was a real appetite to experience the real Africa and produce fresh and exciting copy, and we were able to choose our travel companions both for their ability to deliver powerful features and their entertaining company.

As a result, glowing travel pieces appeared in all the most important newspapers and magazines. Zambia took its place as one of the world's premium safari destinations.

QZ was a delightful if mercurial client. The main challenge was that its single Boeing 707 could be pulled out of intercontinental service at a moment's notice if the then President, Kenneth Kaunda, or KK, needed to use it. This could mean that, as often as not, our QZ press trips would fly on a plane leased from the airline British Midland, which meant the 'Welcome aboard this Zambia Airways flight to Lusaka' announcement left everyone rather puzzled.

This notwithstanding, we were truly blessed. We arrived in Zambia almost before everyone else, when tourism was in its infancy. In those halcyon days you never saw another vehicle in the parks. We were the only people standing on the edge of Vic Falls in full flood or catching a glimpse of the beautiful and elusive sitatunga, the African antelopes that dwell in the marshes, on a misty early morning in the Bangweulu Swamps. We could watch lion cubs at play while their mother looked on with a watchful eye without having to share our experience with jostling jeeps or zebra-striped minibuses. And we witnessed the sunset flight of millions of fruit bats in Kasanka National Park with only the sounds of the bush as accompaniment.

Each day began with a walk at daybreak and finished with a sundowner in a place of extraordinary beauty. We would set off in the Land Rover in the late afternoon, stopping for G&Ts as the sun was setting to enjoy the magnificence of a big African sky, and then pick out the nocturnal animals by search light as we returned to our camp site. We were thrilled to spot the rarely seen snuffling, snouted aardvark, a name I've always remembered as it's the first word in the English dictionary.

On our arrival at Lusaka Airport, a small, slightly cranky Zambia Airways plane would take us to Mfuwe Airfield in the Luangwa Valley. A tarmac strip and a windsock. Arrivals and departures were always fluid and we could sit for hours waiting for a plane that appeared to run to no schedule, or the vehicle to take us to our camp. The place was bereft of information, and we were forced to devise our own entertainment to fill whatever time it might take before the drone of an engine signalled the arrival of our transport. Depending on our travelling companions, we turned to Scrabble, even Scrabble with Drabble on at least one occasion when the eminent author Dame Margaret Drabble was among Sylvia's band of travellers. Another time everyone took turns to wash their hair under a cold tap for no good reason, and the day Fleet Street's finest cracked into the duty free when the Land Rover to pick them up was delayed will have lingered long in local minds.

In common with many government-run national airlines at that time, and despite increased bookings for safari holidays, Zambia Airways met its demise but thankfully it wasn't the end of Zambia for us, as both the Zambia Tourist Board and EcoSafaris, a specialist tour operator, took us on. EcoSafaris' urbane owner, Peter Moss, was the man to have with you on safari and our most memorable and successful adventures were led by him. He was born in the Punjab but spent his early career as a British Colonial Adviser in the then Northern Rhodesia before becoming a park ranger in Kafue National Park. Peter knew the Zambian bush like the back of his hand and if you had him and his Swiss army knife you were safe, regardless of whether the Land Rover had broken down, got stuck in the mud of the Bangweulu

Swamps or a pride of lions had you in its sights.

Health and Safety legislation was not yet in full flower in those days, or even in bud, certainly in Zambia. Had it been, we'd never have left British soil – how much fun we would have missed. Our trips were packed with excitement, from being held in our aeroplane at gunpoint by soldiers on the tarmac at Lusaka Airport after some smart Alec left a *There's a bomb on board* note in the plane's lavatory, to accelerating away from a charging elephant with inches to spare.

Arriving at the crossing over the Luangwa River one afternoon to find the bridge had been washed away, the intrepid Peter announced we would drive across. First he had to negotiate a forty-five-degree slope down to the fast-moving water, at which point the Land Rover fortunately accepted its new amphibious status, enabling him to take us safely across and up the forty-five-degree slope on the other side. It was definitely a white-knuckle crossing, livened up, as if we needed it, by a few crocs snapping at the 'hull' of the vehicle. I remember one of our number, distinguished historian and author, Piers Brendon, the very finest of company, asking mildly, 'Is this wise?' before speaking for us all by vainly pleading, 'No, Peter, no,' as we desperately clung on.

Another memorable highlight under Peter's aegis was the flight in a four-seater plane from the Bangweulu Swamps to the Luangwa Valley. Some of our party had gone before us and by the time the plane returned, the light was fading. Roger the pilot had to refuel speedily and in his rush to get the petrol flowing, he sucked on the tube too enthusiastically, swallowed some and proceeded to throw up. Not ideal for a pilot flying in the gathering gloom over the

Muchinga Escarpment, tricky at the best of times, hoping to find our destination before nightfall.

In the front seat, Sylvia, never noted as a natural navigator, found herself with a map that resembled something from an upper fifth geography lesson.

'Tell me when we're over the rift and getting close to Chibembe,' Roger instructed Sylvia, but it was immediately clear that her map-reading skills weren't going to save our bacon. We all fell back on the age-old technique used by travellers over the ages of 'looking out' for the fire lit by the advance party to mark our landing spot.

Suddenly there it was, and the little plane circled a couple of times before touching down. Strangely, neither of us has any memory of being scared, even though it was touch-and-go. But then we can never remember being scared of anything, however alarming, in Africa. Brian Jackman, for many years *The Sunday Times* Africa guru, who's been on more safaris and in more tight corners with furious wildlife than almost anyone else, still recalls the experience with a fair degree of horror:

'The pilot ended up in the *Guinness Book of Records* as the one who had survived the greatest number of crashes.'

It emerged that Roger was a remittance man, something new to us and a lifestyle choice imposed on him by his desperate parents, who sent regular payments to make sure he stayed away. According to Peter, Africa was full of remittance men.

We stayed in beautiful camps, sometimes under canvas or even in the open under mozzie nets. Those were simpler days and Nsefu, Chibembe, Chinzombo, Chikoko, Kasansanya and Kasanka were comfortable and clean but they weren't luxurious in the way that today's safari camps are. And they were all the better for it. Sometimes they had an en-suite bathroom, but other times we would totter to the long drop with a candle and hope that a hippo wouldn't rush from the undergrowth and catch us at an inconvenient moment.

At that time I was a relentless and hard-to-manage sleepwalker, a hangover from schooldays, which was risky in the African bush. Sylvia had to lock me in my cabin at night to prevent my stepping out into the jaws of a passing lion while in Lady Macbeth mode. On the occasions when we had to share a room, she would often be shaken awake in the small hours to the tune of, 'Get up, the press are here and the sound system isn't working,' or, '*The Sunday Times* needs pictures *now*,' or whatever was the obsession that night.

Travelling with top journalists meant we got VIP treatment: first-class seats, top safari lodges and the best wildlife experts to lead our game drives. On one visit we received a formal invitation to lunch at State House from President Kenneth Kaunda himself.

State House is magnificent. The beautiful colonial mansion is set in 178 acres of central Lusaka, and our lunch was held in grounds boasting an eighteen-hole golf course and tennis court in which wildlife roamed. KK had just returned from a Commonwealth conference where he'd been vociferous on the importance of enforcing strict sanctions against apartheid South Africa.

After a relatively dry few days – by Fleet Street standards – our little band was glad to see a table of wine. Picking up a bottle, I found myself looking at a Nederburg Paarl Riesling, a 'popular and lively' South African wine. It even had a rand price label!

Our interest in KK's choice of wine and any awkward press questions about price labels were brushed aside when he burst into song, much to the bemusement of the assembled company.

The environment was an important part of our PR work and, as well as promoting tourism to Zambia, we became involved with trying to engage Zambians in the potential benefits of tourism to their lives, for which the wildlife was vital. One of our successful schemes was a wildlife club for UK schools that linked with the Chongololo Club in Zambia, so named after a millipede. The Fish Eagle Club was born, in honour of Zambia's national bird.

It ran an art competition in schools all over Zambia, which was won by two delightful schoolboys, Noor and Patrick. The prize was a holiday in London, flights on QZ, staying with the Zambian High Commissioner in his Hampstead residence and, to our surprise, entertainment by Holder Swan. PR people are the eternal catch-alls for what nobody else picks up. The itinerary included a visit to the Hellfire Caves at West Wycombe in Richard's TVR sports car. Not a success, as the boys saw monsters and ghosts in the darkness. Next, a show at the Palladium. Quite what Noor and Patrick made of their prize, we never established. Thanks to the wonders of Google I have discovered that after graduating from London's prestigious Imperial College, Noor set up a successful motorcycle dealership in South East London, but our paths haven't crossed again.

A highlight of the boys' visit was a photocall at London Zoo with Virginia McKenna and her husband, Bill Travers, to highlight the plight of the elephant Pole Pole (Slowly Slowly in Swahili), who'd featured in their film *An Elephant Called Slowly*, and had been gifted to the zoo by the Kenyan

Government, despite Bill and Virginia's objections. It was a very moving encounter: Pole Pole recognised them and stretched out her trunk. She was distressed in her captivity and we all hoped the publicity would enable her to move to a more suitable facility. Sadly, that failed and she had to be put down when she was injured while being relocated to Whipsnade Zoo. Bill, Virginia and their son Will set up The Born Free Foundation in 1984, an international charity that opposes keeping wild animals in captivity and campaigns to keep wildlife in the wild.

We staged an art exhibition at QZ's smart showroom on Piccadilly which was surprisingly successful and had good support here from people like the famous wildlife artist, David Shepherd, and TV personality, David Bellamy. Rolf Harris too – before we knew.

CHAPTER 14

HOME AND AWAY

by Sylvia

In 1987, Lindsay and I got itchy feet to move offices. Some ten years into our Parkway office tenure, we spotted an office for rent in Chalk Farm, a few minutes' walk from Camden Town. We were perfectly happy where we were but couldn't resist having a look. It was opposite the Roundhouse, the world-famous theatre, concert and arts venue. Getting to it was rather *Alice in Wonderland*-ish. The approach didn't fill us with confidence: an unexpected gloomy tunnel from Chalk Farm Road to the back of the Victorian terrace of shops and flats. But then, eureka! We emerged into a beautiful courtyard garden, laid out as a parterre with lavender-lined gravel paths and flower-filled urns. Our office-to-be was the most delightful two-floor farmhouse. The landlord told us that it had been the studio of the artist Walter Sickert, but Sickert or no Sickert we were hooked. It had just what we needed: four rooms on the upper floor for us and a spacious self-contained ground-floor office, which we let. Lindsay and I shared the enormous main room which had been used as the granary. The floor-to-ceiling doors opened out to the courtyard with one of those hooks you see in Dutch paintings. We could sit on the floor and dangle our legs below. Not now, I suspect. Health and Safety has doubtless put paid to that.

Between carting boxes of files the half mile between Parkway and Chalk Farm and keeping the clients happy, I finally got married. My peripatetic life style had been ideal for my chosen bachelor girl status and the easy-come, easy-go boyfriend relationships I enjoyed. The ticking biological clock hadn't bothered me but now, roots firmly back in London, was it time to settle down? I had one quite serious relationship which might have ended in wedding bells, but it came to an end to be replaced by a very strong friendship.

I was already in my early forties when I met Derek. He was three years older than me, divorced with two grown-up children. There were no eyes meeting across a crowded room though a crowded room it was: a drinks reception for supporters of a medical charity. I knew no one there, he knew no one there, so we started chatting together. It was a slow burn. We knew each other for five years before we tied the knot, but lived together for most of them. There were a few estrangements in that time and I should have seen the light, but didn't.

Having been together for so long before we married, we should have realised that compatibility was not our strong suit. This marriage was not made in heaven and, sadly, we went our separate ways after eight years. We never divorced and in fact became better friends when we were under separate roofs and even went on holiday together sometimes. His retirement years were spent mostly in Thailand and it was there, a few days after his seventy-fifth birthday, that he suffered a sudden and fatal aneurism, a shock and sadness for all his family and friends.

I was and remain sad that my choice of husband was so wrong. We should both have realised that we were incompatible and found happiness with the right partners.

I do envy those in loving, easy, happy relationships, but life has been wonderful to me on most fronts and there are bound to be a few regrets along the way.

★★★

Thanks to Zambia Airways, by 1982 we had built up a good contact list and a reputation for travel PR and so other travel clients followed. We would both go on familiarisation trips but then, as a general rule, one or other of us would look after the account. Press trips to Zambia were the exception as neither of us wanted to be left behind, so the Empire was put in the rather querulous hands of our staff who fluctuated over the years but generally consisted of one or more account executives and a secretary. They were augmented by various freelancers with whatever skills we needed at the time, plus the Callback team, who ran our answering service, of which more later. There were no mobiles then, or indeed any form of communication, but the Emp survived, as did they.

India, Mexico and Iceland were among our favourites, though I could have done without one of my press trips to Mexico with six journalists in tow. We all got food poisoning, a couple suffered from altitude sickness and my passport was stolen in a market. The British Embassy in Mexico City told me that Our Man in Merida would fix me up with the necessary travel documents but having dragged my posse to the Consulate there, we found it barred and bolted – Our Man was on a visit to Mexico City. The only alternative was the Embassy itself on our way home, but our plane didn't arrive in Mexico City until 5 p.m. and our London flight was at 7 a.m. the next day. Happily, Her Majesty's British

Embassy came up trumps and stayed open until I arrived well into the evening. I wonder if that would happen these days?

Our involvement in the environment also included being co-ordinating editors for *Mazingira*, the United Nations Environment Programme's academic journal. It came through John Sarsfield, one of my former and most endearing boyfriends who worked with the Emp in various incarnations as film-maker, editor, playwright and even at one stage, sandwich bar manager. John had been asked to help by his sister-in-law, Mairuth Sarsfield, a well-known figure in the environment based in Nairobi. What a coup! It was a completely new challenge for us but we threw ourselves into it enthusiastically. The editor was a hugely respected Oxford academic. We met infrequently but when we did, we were always disconcerted by the pink fluffy mules he wore to receive us. I have a memory, unconfirmed, that they had bunny rabbits on them.

We were invited to bid to take over the publishing of *Mazingira*, but after a colossal effort to put the bid together we discovered the job was already earmarked for an ex-UNEP man going out on his own. It was an inside job and we were just making up the numbers. Having stitched us up, Mairuth's letter giving us the bad news, which arrived on Christmas Eve, ill-advisedly signed off *PS Missing you*. We boiled over at the politics, injustice and time wasted, and the draft of our terse reply included a very schoolgirlish *PS Hope you die soon*, which amused us and cheered us. But we forgot to remove it in the fair copy. Easily done but tricky at the time. Mairuth lived for another thirty-three years so our consciences are clear.

Another of our travel clients, much closer to home, in fact it *was* home, was the English Tourist Board. Showing off the delights of our south coast seaside resorts in a howling gale may not have the allure of watching a herd of elephants at a watering hole, but the ETB did some interesting work. This was Lindsay's bag, which she enjoyed workwise and being close to her home in west London was a plus now that her family was expanding.

I held the ETB reins for the brief time she had off for Georgina's birth and looked after the *England for Excellence* awards, which highlighted the high standard of hospitality in the country, from small B&Bs to stately homes open to the public. One of the prize-winners at the awards dinner at Grosvenor House was Chatsworth, the seat of the Duke of Devonshire and it was my luck to sit next to the then heir apparent, Peregrine (but mercifully known by his nickname, Stoker) Cavendish.

Rather than wear my PR hat and endeavour to talk intelligently about the innovations that led to Chatsworth's award, I took the opportunity to quiz him about the Mitfords, the deliciously aristocratic and eccentric family that has fascinated me all my life. His mother, Deborah, known as Debo, was the youngest of the six Mitford girls, whose sisters included Diana, wife of Sir Oswald Moseley, the Fascists' leader, Jessica, the dyed-in-the-wool Communist, Hitler-loving Unity and the eminent novelist, Nancy. Debo and Pamela were the only 'normal' sisters. Stoker was a delightful dinner companion and seemed to enjoy talking about his eccentric in-laws.

CHAPTER 15

DRAMA IN CHICHESTER

by Sylvia

The Mitfords were to feature in our lives again when we took on the PR for the world-famous Chichester Festival Theatre in 1982. The excitement at landing this plum account was on a par with Zambia Airways. We already had a theatre client, the excellent Belgrade Theatre in Coventry, and when its administrative director, Keith Green, moved to Chichester, we were invited to pitch for the account. Yet again, there wasn't much 'pitching' as our appointment was a cloak-and-dagger affair: a clandestine meeting with Keith and Paul Rogerson, the general manager, at a motel on the fringes of Chichester. Presumably, the then incumbents were not aware of their imminent dismissal. Our successful afternoon was followed by a performance of *The Mitford Girls*, starring Patricia Hodge, which transferred to the West End. And we actually got to meet a Mitford as Diana, Lady Mosley, still beautiful in old age, and her son Max were in the audience.

Our drive home that night was somewhat eventful. We were used to driving in London where many petrol stations were open all night. Not so in West Sussex. Every one of them was in darkness and the petrol gauge had dropped beyond zero. The only sign of life was at a police station (those were the days), so we stopped there and approached the reception desk.

'Good evening, Officer,' I ventured. 'We wondered if you could help us out with some petrol just to get us back to London? We're happy to pay, of course. The tank is past empty.'

One of the policemen manning the desk gave me a wary look. 'I'm afraid we're not allowed to give or sell petrol to the public,' he replied, glancing at his colleague.

'But what are we to do?' Lindsay intervened in a pleading voice. 'We've come all the way from Chichester and nothing is open.'

We had them between a rock and a hard place as they couldn't abandon us to our certain fate. While they pondered the problem, they invited us to sit in their back room where we happily watched the rerun of that famous day's Ashes match at Headingley when Ian Botham and Bob Willis snatched victory from the jaws of defeat. Then we were on our way to London – sworn to secrecy.

Every first night saw us in the fully-fuelled purple Mini hurtling up and down the A3 to Chichester, usually with the adorable Jack Tinker, drama critic of the *Daily Mail,* with us on the return journey. Jack was a legend in his lifetime: a diminutive and flamboyant character, the most popular of the London critics. This is not to say he always wrote kindly in his reviews; indeed, he could be savage but always fair. He was a born raconteur and we would happily have driven all the way to Scotland for his inexhaustible supply of hilarious tales, often featuring Princess Margaret.[6]

How different life was then. It's hard to believe that we had to stop en route at a telephone box for Jack to check

6 Sadly Jack died of a heart attack when he was just fifty-eight. That night the West End theatre lights were dimmed in his honour, a gesture normally reserved for actors alone.

if the copytaker had any queries about the copy he had filed before leaving the theatre. Also difficult to believe is that I had to rise at dawn the next day to go to King's Cross station, one of the few places selling the first editions of the newspapers carrying the reviews. I then put them on the train to Chichester, the only way in those days of getting the reviews to the theatre promptly.

Chichester was an unmitigated joy. Patrick Garland had just become Artistic Director and the plays in the 1982 twenty-first birthday season made the West End look almost provincial. But we were picking up at a crucial time. After the heady early years with Laurence Olivier as its Artistic Director, the theatre had slumped to the point that it was no longer attracting Fleet Street's top theatre critics to its first nights. It was our job to reverse that situation and we were helped by it being its twenty-first birthday and the calibre of plays for the season. These included Joan Plowright in *Cavell*, the story of the WW1 nurse; and John Mills in *Goodbye, Mr Chips*. Sandy Wilson's *Valmouth* had the same cast – Bertice Reading, Fenella Fielding and Doris Hare – as in the original London production twenty-two years earlier, and was scheduled for a *Sunday Times Magazine* front cover, pictures by Lord Snowdon, Princess Margaret's hugely respected photographer husband. What a coup – but alas there was a change of picture editor and the piece was 'spiked', meaning the paper had decided not to run it – newspapers in those days used to have an actual spike for the purpose.

Except you don't spike photos taken by Snowdon.

His understandable ire resulted in a later, albeit inside, piece. Not quite the same, but better than nothing.

As far as we were concerned, our early efforts were

going as swimmingly as they should have been. This account was a PR's dream and we were busy placing stories to appear to coincide with the birthday when we were summoned to the Royal Overseas League for a board meeting. We went along cheerfully, expecting the assembled company to want an update. Instead we were met by extraordinary aggression. There were some fifteen board members present and they were less than welcoming.

The chairman glowered at us. 'You've been in this job for four weeks now and we haven't seen anything in the papers. This is very disappointing.'

Oops, this was unexpected. 'We have masses of stories in the pipeline, but it takes time between negotiating a story and seeing it in print,' I tried to explain. 'And we want most of them to coincide with the actual birthday'.

He was not mollified.

Hugh Cudlipp, the legendary Cudlipp of the *Mirror*, was on the Chichester board so I charged headlong in. 'Lord Cudlipp, can we appeal to you to back us up?'

'Fight your own battles,' he replied gruffly but not unkindly. 'You're doing fine.'

There were no more complaints. The mere utterance by Lord C had swung opinion in our favour and we went on to do a further six seasons. The chairman had the grace to acknowledge the publicity that came pouring in.

Lord Cudlipp had been a brilliant, if fierce, editor, but in retirement he'd become something of a pussycat. One evening he entertained Lindsay and me with industrial quantities of gin in the House of Lords bar, sending us tottering into the Westminster night with a box of House of Lords chocolates.

A very dear man.

The annual press conference we organised in London took place in the Martini Terrace on the eighteenth floor of New Zealand House in the Haymarket – Martini was a sponsor then. It was always a slightly nerve-wracking event as it was attended by all the stars of that season's productions, with a battery of photographers, reporters, TV crews and drama critics all keen for a slice of the action. They included such stars as Diana Rigg, Alan Bates, Maggie Smith, Joan Plowright, John Mills, Suzy Quatro, Googie Withers, Joanna Lumley, Penelope Keith and even Dr Zhivago himself, Omar Sharif.

I can claim to have dined with Omar but not, alas, *à deux*. There were ten of us at the Dorchester, organised by the theatre, and I could well understand why he had such an image as a heart-throb. He was charming, charismatic, handsome and oozed sex appeal.

All the actors we met at Chichester were easy going and friendly, but my favourite was Patricia Hodge. Lindsay and I arranged a fair few press interviews for our leading actors, which they loved, but Patricia was the only one who bothered to come over to me in the Green Room and thank me personally.

★★★

It was around this time that Aids/HIV appeared from nowhere and was to strike terror in the hearts of gay men particularly, but not exclusively. It was to kill thousands and included two people we worked with closely, a very sad time. One of our clients was a top London restaurant with a delightful manager who became a good friend of ours. Alas, he was struck down with the dreaded disease and died while still in his early thirties, as did our printer friend who took care of all the printing jobs we undertook for our clients.

CHAPTER 16

EVERYTHING IN THE GARDEN IS ROSY

by Lindsay

It was never a conscious decision for the Emp to specialise in travel and arts PR, but that's what happened and it suited us just fine. It meant we were able go to some of the world's most wonderful places and have the best seats in the house.

We certainly hadn't envisaged branching into horticulture, but in 1991 I met Jeff Morrison, a well-known event organiser, at MOOT, the English Tourist Board's travel and tourism exhibition. Jeff was there to promote the fledgling Hampton Court Palace International Flower Show, or HCPIFS, as it was not so snappily known, which was giving the world-famous Chelsea Flower Show a run for its money and ruffling the feathers of the mighty Royal Horticultural Society.

The Show was the brainchild of Adrian Boyd, who lived in nearby Thames Ditton and spotted the potential of the gorgeous Home Park of Hampton Court Palace for such an event. He persuaded the palace, whose government funding had been cut in yet another government restructuring, that this would be a great boost to revenue. At the same time, Network South East, which operated the trains around Greater London and beyond, agreed to sponsor it to the tune of £750,000 a year. A coup indeed.

The first Show took place in 1990 and was well received. Visitors travelled on special trains run between Waterloo and Hampton Court, welcomed at each end by staff wearing carnations. But it needed more visitors and a much bigger media profile.

Ebullient straight talker Jeff and I hit it off. It turned out HCPIFS was on the lookout for a PR consultancy. My ears pricked up.

'Look no further!' I said jauntily, more in hope than anything else. This was a prestigious account and competition would be super-keen.

Jeff produced his business card and a meeting was fixed within days, although it took quite a lot longer to clinch the deal. HCPIFS was a fabulous feather in the Emp's cap and we have often wondered why we succeeded against the competition. We think it was probably to do with quirkiness – ours and theirs. They were delightfully off the wall.

Adrian Boyd was the typical nineties ad man: original, entrepreneurial and charming. One summer morning before the Show opened, I remember him cruising beside the Long Water at Hampton Court in his gold Rolls Royce, vodka to hand.

Another Adrian, Adrian Greenoak, or 'Greenfly' to us, was the horticultural genius behind the Show. He was a one-off, very likeable and good company. Wildly creative, a pianist, composer, poet and fully paid-up eccentric, he was never seen without his dark suit and bow tie, whatever the weather or occasion. In the build-up to the Show, Adrian would set up house in a caravan on the site from which he worked day and night to pull off the colossal horticultural feat. Taking his piano with him, he retired to Crete after leaving the RHS, presumably still clad in suit and bow tie, emerging for a spell to set up the Adelaide Rose Festival.[7]

Our first HCPIFS was in 1992. The Queen opened the Network South East show garden, the Queen Mother came and Sylvia and I held court in a splendid swag-lined press tent, filled by a curious and generally positive press. Richard, Ben and Georgy – and even Jessie Dog – all joined the build-up and breakdown. Our transition into horticultural PR went very well indeed.

The news came later in the year that Network South East was withdrawing its sponsorship. This was a serious shock. Hampton Court Palace put the Show out to tender and the RHS won the sealed bids.

It was particularly hard for Adrian Boyd, who lost everything he'd created in a moment. Greenfly and Jeff were both taken on by the RHS after the *putsch* and happily they took us with them. They did everything they could to help us, luring Sylvia and me to a secret meeting at a seedy pub in Horseferry Road, known thereafter as the Badger's Bottom, to plot how to navigate the politics.

And there were plenty of politics. Getting the account was one thing; convincing the RHS marketing and PR team that their new baby was in good hands was another. Our first meeting took place in the grand RHS boardroom at Vincent Square and it's fair to say they were less than thrilled to find themselves having to work with us. They were most unfriendly and tried to trip us up constantly, which puzzled us until we realised they wanted to do the PR themselves and resented our involvement. It all worked out in the end, a *modus vivendi* was found and for the next seven summers, Sylvia and I focused our attention on all things horticultural.

7 Sadly, both Adrians died far too young at sixty-five.

The Show, now renamed the Hampton Court Garden Festival, was much more spacious and relaxed than Chelsea and very much more fun. It was and still is spectacular. Spread over thirty-four acres of the Palace's Home Park on either side of the Long Water, it attracts some 140,000 visitors each year and features show gardens, floral marquees, a rose tent and hundreds of trade stands. The RHS was able to bag the *Daily Mail* as a sponsor, and its huge, themed pavilion and a competition to win a 'Dream Cottage' became a big attraction.

Sylvia and I loved our week at the Show each year, hectic though it was. Our press tent grew into a press marquee, over which we reigned from 7.30 a.m. to 9 p.m. every day. On our initiative, it featured a roof terrace where the press congregated with a view over the marquees and gardens to Hampton Court Palace and the Long Water. The Show attracted media from all over the world as well as celebrities, many of whom came to the annual Celebrity Lunch Sylvia hosted. The evergreen and charming Cliff Richard and Gloria Hunniford were our mainstays and were always willing to help with opening gardens and joining photocalls. Members of Cliff's enormous fan club came too, or tried to. They used to dedicate themselves to finding ever more bold and imaginative ways to blag their way in on Press Day before the Show opened to the public. Our job was to deter them. As the day drew closer, we'd get all kinds of calls from people claiming to be gardening writers demanding a press ticket. From the crack of dawn, they would leap out from behind marquees and floral displays to get a glimpse of their hero. Age and mobility were no barrier.

It was extraordinary.

On the first public day of the first year of the RHS running the Show, we stood with the Head of Marketing, Charles Mills, to watch the crowds pouring through the turnstiles at opening time.

The time came, the time went and only a few people had trickled through.

'I'm deeply depressed,' said Charles, giving us a sideways 'it's all your fault' look.

Suddenly, a massive crowd appeared and surged through the gates – and continued to arrive in their thousands.

Charles's 'deeply depressed' remark has never been forgotten. Abbreviated to DD, it entered the Emp's exclusive and extensive lexicon, and has been used repeatedly when things are going awry.

After eight happy but exhausting years, we decided that 1999 would be our last Show. Sylvia had moved to the coast and Ben and Georgy were growing up fast and needed their mother around more. People didn't work from home then, or very few did but it was possible – just – through the wonders of faxes, personal computers, mobile phones and the advent of email. It meant I was able to be at home during the children's teenage years.

Excitingly, the 1999 Show was recorded for posterity in a feature film, *Greenfingers*, starring Helen Mirren, Clive Owen and the now ubiquitous Danny Dyer in his early years, with Sting's wife Trudie Styler as executive producer. It was based on the true story of an award-winning Hampton Court show garden created by prisoners from HMP Leyhill which had been featured in *The New York Times*, where it was spotted by a group of young American producers, directors and writers.

I found myself facilitating the making of *Greenfingers*, becoming involved with the various stages of its production and to my astonishment, I was asked to read for the part of myself, namely the film's publicist. I duly turned up at the offices of the distinguished casting director Michelle Guish opposite Liberty, read and was cast. It was a speaking part, which had me popping up in a few scenes, including with the blessed Dame Helen. I even had my own Winnebago on set and the attentions of costume and make-up departments.

Such glamour!

Disappointingly, my appearance wasn't followed by a call from Mr Spielberg.

Sylvia and I attended the premiere, which unfortunately took place the night before 9/11 and *Greenfingers* didn't fly as we'd all hoped. I may be biased but it's a super film and the music by Sting, Elton, Bruce Springsteen and others was fantastic. It's still available on Amazon and crops up on television from time to time all these years later. Richard watched it on a BA flight from Tehran, on the homeward leg of a business trip, not long after it came out. In those days, a single movie was shown onboard and when I picked him up at the airport, I was a bit of a celeb with his fellow travellers.

Having Hampton Court as a client allowed us to extend what might – possibly a little misleadingly – be described as our horticultural practice. First to sign up was garden designer Duncan Heather, then a callow twenty-one-year-old and the *enfant terrible* of the gardening world. His very first show garden won Best in Show at Hampton Court. Apart from being precociously talented, he never shied away from a controversial comment, which was helpful to the publicity effort.

We met the venerable Rosemary Alexander, principal of the frightfully smart English Gardening School, when she attended one of the 'How to do your own PR' seminars we'd developed as a sideline to the main consultancy. She promptly decided she'd rather we did it for her and so began a long, if patchy and not always harmonious, association. Every so often she'd sack us but then decide she needed some PR and back we'd go. Throughout everything, whether or not we were in favour, Sylvia gave regular talks to the students on how to do the PR for their fledgling garden design businesses.

Since then I've done a lot of gardening PR, particularly relating to its benefits to wellbeing and some, like the *Greenfingers* story, has involved prisoners. Over the years I have been in and out of many prisons – from Edinburgh to Wormwood Scrubs and the infamous HMP Wandsworth, where I was involved in The Conservation Foundation's 'Unlocking Nature' project to create green spaces behind those grim walls. Very satisfyingly it helped quite a few prisoners find their own green fingers.

CHAPTER 17

GLITZ, GLAMOUR AND THE MONA LISA

by Lindsay

Apart from our theatre and travel clients and the odd foray into fashion, including for Moss Bros, the Emp took on several clients in the visual arts.

Charles de Temple was a jewellery designer, a pioneering figurehead of the modernist movement. His bold, beautiful abstract jewellery was, and still is, in high demand. The illegitimate son of the American cowboy film star Tom Mix, he'd spent his early years in a Mexican circus before taking London by storm.

Charles's exquisite 'gallery' was in Piccadilly Arcade, just off Jermyn Street. It was seriously over-the-top opulent. Upstairs it was all grey suede-lined walls and glittering jewellery but below stairs it was more homely. I have a memory of a McVitie's biscuit tin filled with precious stones alongside smoked salmon sandwiches being knocked up for the weekly celebrity salons. When I had to take pieces of jewellery worth tens of thousands of pounds for viewing to the hallowed halls of *Vogue* or to a photoshoot, rather than it being securely strapped unseen to my body, the swag was bundled into a Ryman's bag for me to walk or take a tube to my destination.

Every week there was a lunchtime salon to which

celebs would be invited, together with the press. A Thursday guest list might include the likes of Joan Collins, Roger Moore, possibly the most famous of the 007s and Lady Diana Cooper, in her heyday considered to be the most beautiful woman in England and still putting on a good show at 88. Even the odd politician and minor European royalty. Whoever was in town for a premiere, party or book launch would be entertained to smoked salmon, champagne, harp music and some eclectic company. One exciting day Elton John stopped by and left with bags of beautiful things.

With his Karl Lagerfeld ponytail and astonishing tantrums which often boiled up unexpectedly but disappeared just as quickly, Charles was always a surprising and terrifying client. But it was his fellow director, Carol, who proved to have the biggest surprise up her sleeve.

After we had gone our separate ways, we were startled to hear that Carol, a pillar of respectability, had cooked up a cunning plan to recall clients' jewellery, ostensibly for a Charles de Temple retrospective. Back it all came, the owners more than happy to envisage their treasured jewels in an exhibition. And off Carol went to the pawnbrokers and put it all in hock. We were told that she pocketed the proceeds, left the redemption slips and legged it to America! Quite a stunt for which we had grudging admiration.

Our Charles de Temple credentials led to us being taken on by a wealthy man who'd acquired the licence to produce memorabilia of the visit of Pope John II to Ireland in 1979 and was convinced he would make yet more millions. The coat of arms on the commemorative plate, glasses and crystal bell was designed by Archbishop Bruno B Heim, the apostolic delegate who was the Vatican's top man on ecclesiastical heraldry. How could it not be a sell-out?

We didn't share his confidence and told him as much over the many late evenings of meetings at his splendid Highgate house. But he was not to be discouraged. Unfortunately for him we were proved right and it ended badly.

Around this time, we found ourselves promoting a sculptor. Jon Douglas was self-taught and talented but he was no Michelangelo or Rodin. His subjects were popular rather than classical – he'd previously been commissioned to make a sculpture of Elvis by the owner of Elvisly Yours, a chain of shops selling Elvis Presley memorabilia in London. Jon's lifelong dream had been to recreate the *Mona Lisa* in 3D, to reveal the Gioconda's profile as no one had ever done before. The PR part wasn't easy as the art press, to which Jon aspired, was super sniffy, declaiming it as 'Not really art'. Nevertheless, we persevered and succeeded in getting the sculpture installed in the foyer of the Savoy. Jon was thrilled and insisted on giving us shares in *Mona*, who was on sale for a cool but ambitious million pounds. Just as well for Sylvia that there were no million pound offers as the share certificate was lost in one of her monster spring-cleaning sessions. That could have been the end of a beautiful friendship. We lost touch with Jon too, which was a pity, as he was a lovely man.

Not surprisingly, given Sylvia's hotel background, hotels featured extensively in our portfolio. Other than Rank Hotels and Trusthouse Forte, most of our hotel clients were independent bijou properties scattered around the country, which covered a pretty big area – from Cardiff to Mull, Devon to Yorkshire and several places in between.

Then there were the clients that didn't fit into any particular box but provided much unexpected delight. One such was SuperTed, the ursine children's cartoon superhero whose first language was Welsh and who was a force for good in a thoroughly bad world. He was in a way a happy link to our earlier South African Wombling adventures, but I wasn't sorry that this time the job didn't involve dressing up in another hot and smelly 'skin'.

CHAPTER 18

I'VE GOT AN IDEA, SWAN

by Lindsay

PR can be precarious at the best of times and so it was important to have another string to our bow, indeed strings, when the inevitable recessions hit. And hit they did in the eighties and nineties. We tackled these with a combination of practising what we preached by pitching for press coverage for the Emp and falling back on a heady mix of entrepreneurial ideas. All, without exception, *Sylvia's* mix of entrepreneurial ideas.

On the press front, two instances – both major triumphs – come to mind. One was a piece in *The Times* with the headline *Empress of All She Surveys*, under which a beaming picture of Sylvia and me was accompanied by the story of the Emp and its wildly eclectic sidelines that kept us afloat through thick and thin. My mother, not given to gratuitous – or indeed any other – praise, declared it her 'finest hour' when the feature came to the attention of her hairdresser's other clients during her weekly shampoo and set.

In those days, a newspaper story always had an immediate effect. Not so now. After *The Times* piece, the Emp's phones rang off the hook and all manner of good things came our way. There were enquiries from potential clients, including from a hotel on the edge of Windsor

Great Park run by a mysterious sect, which took us on then promptly ran out of money. The piece recounted our South Africa story and was duly picked up by a Johannesburg newspaper, which finished the tale of Wombles and Taylor Burton with a startling (mis)quote from Sylvia: '... and then we got married.' A surprise to everyone. However, as a result, Laura, a British journalist who'd been plotting her exit from SA, got in touch and came to work with us on her return. She proved to be worth her weight in gold.

Easily the most successful sideline was our 'How to do your own PR' seminars. These were given a huge boost by a big feature in the *Financial Times*, accompanied by a suitably serious photograph of us both. This brought the most extraordinary number of enquiries from all over, including Europe and even Moscow, after which *The Times* ran the story *PR Service Finds a Market in Moscow*. We also found our way onto *Woman's Hour* and into various newspapers and magazines, including *The Bulletin*, an English-language Brussels magazine, which brought enquiries from Belgium. As well as being satisfying evidence of how PR spins, it was a change to be the beneficiaries, rather than the instigators, of media coverage. We rather enjoyed our time in the spotlight.

Based on something we'd developed for the English Tourist Board, our seminars passed on the tricks of the PR trade to small and not so small businesses. At one time we were conducting two sessions a week for eight people around the huge partners' desk in our lovely Chalk Farm farmhouse, as well as the odd tailor-made event for companies. They became a fantastic source of income.

Unexpectedly, the seminars also brought in a varied group of new clients like the aforementioned Rosemary

Alexander who, having heard our pearls of wisdom, decided they didn't want to do their own PR and it would be better to pay us to do it. We met some interesting people and companies that way.

Before Lonely Hearts columns in newspapers and then online dating, marriage bureaux were the only way to seek an arranged meeting with the opposite sex. (Same sex partnerships were unlikely to have been on offer at that time). The queen of them all was Hedi Fisher who happened to be at the same seminar as Rosemary. She was quick off the mark to ask Hedi if she had a suitable man for her daughter who was reluctant to leave the comforts of home. History doesn't relate if true love was lurking in Hedi's fat files of love seekers.

Not all Sylvia's ideas enjoyed the same success. I came to dread Monday mornings, as she would inevitably arrive refreshed from the weekend with yet another scheme to transform the Emp's bank balance. Take your pick: as well as the PR seminars we had a telephone answering service, a greeting cards company, a share-a-secretary scheme and Homes in England for wealthy Hong Kongites. Some were wonderful money spinners, others less so, however, they were all eclipsed by the Fleet Sandwich Bar.

One Monday morning towards the end of 1980 I was innocently picking up the answerphone messages and going through the post when Sylvia breezed in, grinning from ear to ear.

'I've got an idea, Swan,' she said.

Cruising down Farringdon Street in her beloved purple Mini that weekend she'd spotted a *To Let* sign above a sandwich bar near Ludgate Circus. It piqued all her entrepreneurial instincts.

'It's got the *best* location a matter of yards from St Paul's, just along from Fleet Street,' she enthused. 'There are offices everywhere and, best of all, no other sandwich bars in sight.' To her, the opportunity was irresistible. 'We'll do it up and come up with a super menu – not just sarnies but hot meals, tasty soup and Justin de Blank bread.'[8]

The Fleet stood on the corner of Fleet Lane, not far from Ludgate Circus and Fleet Street. Behind a low wall in its dark, damp and displeasing basement ran the ancient River Fleet itself. Upstairs was the Coreen Munt Employment Agency. While Coreen's parents had clearly been unaware of the perils of spoonerisms, her name afforded many hours of simple delight to the sandwich makers below.

With the help of Mr Campbell, Sylvia's most favourite DIY expert and Richard, we tarted up the Fleet. We tarted up the menu, too. Our Justin de Blank sandwiches had a range of irresistible fillings. There was a menu of home-cooked fare and the Fleet's greasy spoon days were consigned to history.

On Sundays we would create gallons of home-made soups and tons of shepherds' pies for the week ahead and drive it from Isleworth, where Richard and I were living, to the Fleet. Sylvia made a parallel journey from Hampstead.

Things started badly when the incumbent manager legged it to Spain with the takings. I spotted him when we were waiting at Malaga Airport for the flight home after Richard's sister's wedding, where it transpired he'd set up a hire car business. Staffing became a nightmare and, in the end, we fell back on friends with the girlfriend of a Callback photographer client and dear John Sarsfield filling the breach.

8 Justin de Blank was a fine food pioneer who made delicious bread.

Sylvia had been right about the location, as the Royal Wedding was to prove. It was big for Charles and Diana, as well as the rest of the world. It was huge for the Fleet, located as it was within a few yards of the route and St Paul's itself. We made and froze hundreds of sandwiches and recruited a group of sales persons – mainly Sylvia's nieces and their friends – who took out supplies in those trays that cinema cigarette girls used to wear. It was not resoundingly successful as the sales team became distracted, but it was enormous fun to be part of history.

Even with our posh bread and homemade fare the Fleet just wasn't a goer. It stood somewhere between a greasy spoon and the new wave of sandwich bars and, with a short lease and awkward staff, there was no point in investing in it.

We sold the rest of the lease but when it expired, the bulldozers moved in and Coreen and the other occupants of the building dispersed. We were sorry but our sorrow was mitigated by enormous relief.

Our greeting cards company, Gloucester Gate Productions, satisfied Sylvia's creative urges up to but definitely not including the final artwork. A perky, or possibly cringeworthy, line dreamt up by one or other of us, was brought to life by an animal cartoon such as 'I'm udderly lost without you', illustrated by a lugubrious cow, 'Sorry you're not wellephant' with a sad baby elephant covered in spots and 'Just dropping you a lion' with a little lion dropping earthwards. The Christmas range, of which Sylvia was particularly proud, featured Father Christmas and reindeer in London situations. The reindeer always had the upper hoof such as they took the seats on the bus while FC had to strap hang; elsewhere the reindeer sheltered from the rain in a guard's sentry box and FC got wet. They did well in this country and when we went on a government trade delegation to Hong Kong, we picked a large order from the terribly grand Lane Crawford, HK's Harrods.

The trade delegation also enabled us to get 'Homes in England' off the ground. This was a research, buy, do up and let service for the well-heeled Hong Kong Chinese people anxious to move their money into London properties after the UK colony was returned to China. No prizes for whose idea that was. We came away with three clients and Sylvia, who loved poring over the expensive property pages, found three suitable apartments – a huge mansion flat in West Hampstead, a two-storey maisonette in Hyde Park and a quirky top floor place in Belsize Park. They were good buys: we took huge care in decorating and furnishing them and they all did well for their Hong Kong owners.

But they were far from plain sailing.

The West Hampstead property was snapped up immediately at top dollar by an apparently devoted couple. Rent arrived punctually each month and things were progressing smoothly until an urgent call came through from the managing agent for Sylvia. After suggesting she sat down, he delivered the bombshell news.

'Your tenant has murdered his girlfriend.'

By the time we got there the poor woman's body had thankfully been removed, but as it had been a murder scene, we were glad of our Marigolds that day.

The Hyde Park flat was the jewel in the Homes in England crown. It had what estate agents describe as 'original features', notably a magnificent moulded ceiling in the drawing room. We set ourselves up there to keep an eye on the carpet layers above, while simultaneously planning a media campaign. A sudden burst of foul language was followed by a rush of water followed by the beautiful ceiling. Upstairs, a feckless carpet layer had put a nail through a water pipe. We escaped by a whisker but it was bad for our nerves – and the client's.

Not quite top of the range but still in a lovely location, the Belsize Park flat gave us scope for a bolder interior design and was probably our best effort. Plus no one was murdered and the ceiling didn't come down.

No one under the age of forty will have a clue what an answering service is, just as they will never have seen a manual typewriter. It's difficult to believe that in the late seventies and eighties there were no mobiles, very few answering machines and you couldn't divert a call to another landline. The inspiration for Callback came to Sylvia one quiet weekend – the devil makes work for idle hands – but it was actually a good little money-spinner and easy to run. Clients simply gave our Callback number to their contacts and messages could be collected any time from us during office hours.

Callback quickly built up a client list of creatives including film directors, photographers and journalists. The photographer David Bailey's agent was a client and we even had a future Archduchess of Austria on the books for a while. It was during her 'It' girl years and I think it was helpful to her to be able to politely palm off undesirables with a phone number. She didn't pick up the messages. There was also the usual smattering of PRs, the odd plumber, carpet cleaner and pest controller.

Callback was also a *poste restante* and held letters for at least one set of illicit lovers and people who were avoiding creditors, ex-spouses or whatever. The call handlers were interesting and comprised some resting TV actors, including Arabella Weir ('Does My Bum Look Big In This?') and Owen Brenman (Dr Heston Carter in *Doctors* and Victor Meldrew's neighbour in *One Foot In The Grave*). Another, Sue, was a singer who was signed by a record label while working for us and we also had a couple of artists manning the phones and helping with admin. At one very exciting point our offices were used for a police sting. A David Gower – not the cricketer – was engaged in a gold bullion scam which involved fake bank drafts. A succession of charming detectives embedded themselves at the Emp for what seemed like weeks until David was lured in to pick up a large bank transfer, at which point they pounced.

In parallel we ran 'Share-a-Secretary' where we pimped Sue, our secretary at the time, to local businesses that needed letters typed, sorted, filing done. That kind of thing. It was less successful than Callback but handily helped to spread the cost of staff.

In the end, although PR was what we did as our day job, the Emp's sidelines sustained us through the lean times and provided a variety to life and hours of hilarity that we would have otherwise missed.

CHAPTER 19

A WOMAN OF PROPERTY

by Sylvia

'How can you *enjoy* wheeling and dealing in property?' my friends would ask me, mystified how anyone could actually relish the cut and thrust of buying and selling bricks and mortar. How indeed? I obviously inherited the love of it from my dear mama whose aspirations were rather higher than mine, as her portfolio included the purchase of a castle.

I'm an urban girl at heart and I've always loved pounding the streets and, yes, looking at houses of any shape or size but especially those in need of some TLC. And I wanted a piece of the action. As I lived and worked in the Camden area, this was the obvious place to test my entrepreneurial skills in the buying and selling of bricks and mortar. The search began and in 1982 I fell upon a two-bedroom flat in Nassington Road, which is virtually on Hampstead Heath. It was in a bad state but it cost just £40,000.[9] I didn't have £40,000; I didn't even have £400, but this small consideration never stood in my way. Mortgages covered some of the cost but more was needed. I became the queen of borrowing and beetled around my well-off friends banging my begging bowl for money – at a rate of interest which they were more than happy with and still gave me a profit.

9 The smaller flat above it is on the market today for £1,500,000!

I looked only at cheap, unmodernised flats but in good areas and of all the twenty-six flats I acquired over several years, only one cost me more than £100,000. The eighties were a God-given time for such a venture as there was plenty of choice at give-away prices.

Initially I bought, did up and sold in quick succession. Later, when I had a coterie of lenders and even had accumulated some cash myself, I was able to rent the flats so I could indulge in my passion, but not necessarily talent, for design and furniture.

Friday was Red Letter Day in the office for me and Groan Day for Lindsay, as she knew she'd probably soon be rushing off with me to see a flat. It was *Ham & High* day, when the weekly *Hampstead & Highgate Express*, packed full of properties for sale from Hampstead mansions to my end of the market: cheap and cheerful doer-uppers, hit the newsstands. Although Lindsay was not directly involved in my mad pursuit of property, she would gamely join in the search and she and her Marigolds knew every nook and cranny of the flats I bought.

I loved the search, the viewings, the cut and thrust of negotiating the price, planning the changes and improvements to be made and finally selling or renting. I did not enjoy all the legal stuff between me and the seller, and then me and the buyer. Of course, a solicitor looked after all the conveyancing, but the outdated property laws in England always caused my hackles to rise. The time between agreeing a sale and exchange of contracts can run into several months as everything moves at a snail's pace, including the solicitors. Absurdly, either party can pull out at any time without any penalty, right up to the seconds before contracts are exchanged. For those buying their own homes, the disappointment is huge, and often causes the domino effect as chains collapse. No wonder buying and selling property is listed alongside divorce and death as one of the most stressful life events. Nervous breakdown time. The law is an ass.

Riddled with damp and generally in a grim state, a huge four-storey house in Roderick Road at the then unfashionable end of NW3 but yards from Hampstead Heath was a major undertaking. So impressed were Derek and I by its transformation into two maisonettes that we decided to live in the lower one complete with spiral staircase. Bought for £53,000 in 1982, Roderick Road houses now fetch around the £3 million mark.

How lucky my generation was to live at a time when we needed only a small deposit to get onto the property ladder and we were able to be home owners in our twenties or thirties. I'm sorry for today's young people who face a lifetime of renting, or having to stay with mum and dad when they should long since have flown the nest. The mortgage companies don't help, the deposit needed is far too high and the property prices themselves rule out even a studio flat. Life is unnecessarily tough on them.

By and large, the flats I rented rather than sold brought me few problems. There are many tales about tenants leaving their rented flats in appalling condition or doing a midnight flit owing thousands of pounds. I was lucky except for one or two notable cases.

I was indignant when the managing agent of a flat I owned at the Chalk Farm end of Haverstock Hill wrote to let me know that other residents had complained about my tenant 'urinating on the flower beds outside a flat window' and would I please do something about it. I responded tersely, pointing out that it must be a case of mistaken identity as my tenant was a pillar of the community, a doctor at the Royal Free Hospital. When the complaints persisted, I wrote a rather jokey letter to the doctor saying that I was sure he wasn't the guilty party but could he just confirm.

No response.

It was time to investigate. Lindsay came too for moral support as I had no idea what I was going to find.

The locks had been changed but there was a small cupboard by the front door with access both sides, presumably for milk bottles in their time. Despite being eight months pregnant, Lindsay pluckily volunteered to squeeze herself through it and let me in. A dreadful shock awaited us. Let us just say that his random peeing was not confined to flower beds and he also suffered an even worse incontinence problem. The flat was in a disgusting state; the sheets had obviously never been washed. Seeing it was a horrible experience. Despite clearly being in the grip of drink and drugs, my tenant was still tending to the needs of ill people in a leading teaching hospital.

At another flat, the apparently respectable tenant working in the City suddenly upped sticks and was gone. The sleuths were back on another investigation.

This time, every single surface was covered with coins (they totted up to more than £75) and the floor was smothered with thousands of CDs. Most disconcerting was the stack of brochures inviting readers to bondage parties and a dungeon experience in rural Wiltshire. Perhaps that's where my erstwhile tenant had gone.

CHAPTER 20

SUSSEX BY THE SEASIDE

by Sylvia

In 1998 I turned sixty and decided to move to Hove on the south coast next to Brighton. It was on a whim, another of my spur-of-the-moment decisions. Having spent some of my formative years in Sussex, it just seemed like a good idea.

By then life had changed considerably. In 1995 we'd made the decision to sell the Emp and handed over our Chalk Farm Road office lease and our clients to a company which held on to the Holder Swan name for a while. We'd agreed to continue to do the Hampton Court Flower Show PR and I was house-hunting in Hove, while trying to sell my London house. This time was traumatic for me, as I was simultaneously coping with hospital visits following the discovery of cancer after a routine smear test – eventually and thankfully a wrong diagnosis – and, worst of all, desperate about the decline of my much-loved brother, Bob.

Of my siblings, John was the studious one with an Oxford law degree, although what use that was for his subsequent career in marketing I know not. Meanwhile, Bob and academia simply didn't gel. His headmaster remarked that he wasn't merely at the bottom of the B stream, but through it. It seemed not to faze my parents that neither he nor I put in much effort in the classroom and probably rightly so, as we both did okay in the big bad world. Bob became an ace salesman – he could charm the birds off the trees, but wasn't smarmy. For a while he had his own business selling coin-operated snack machines, but as his interest waned, so did his sales and his company didn't survive long.

Unfortunately, over the years Bob had descended into a haze of alcohol. He had fought the monster for a long time and, just as he seemed to be winning, back he slipped.

I took him to see his GP. There was no messing about with her: she went straight for the jugular.

'Unless you stop drinking now, you'll very soon be dead,' she warned him.

Poor Bob. He didn't want to die but the vodka had a tight grip on him. He'd made a bit of a mess of his life in recent years. His wife, Ann, had understandably become an ex-wife and now his lovely long-suffering girlfriend, Sophia, was giving him ultimatums. He was living in a splendid flat right on the Thames in Chelsea, courtesy of The Royal Borough of Kensington and Chelsea, but I was constantly worried that he'd soon be given his marching orders and instead of looking *at* the Embankment, he'd be sleeping *on* it in a cardboard box.

I pleaded with the doctor to find him a drying-out sanctuary and after several phone calls she came up trumps. There was a small place near Great Ormond Street Hospital with a vacancy and before you could say 'Thank God' I was careering along the Embankment with my worse-for-wear passenger. I sang all the way home after dropping him off into the care of a peaceful place with friendly staff. He thrived there and a stone-cold sober Bob emerged back into the world a few weeks later. He wrote me a card, which I still have, promising me he would never, ever drink again.

Sadly, with the best intentions in the world, the vodka bottle proved too big a pull and not so long after his rehabilitation I found him unconscious in his flat. The wonderful paramedics brought him round and transferred him to Westminster Hospital, where they good naturedly gave him the same care as any other patient. He made the same promises when he was discharged but, yet again, the bottle won.

One October day in 1998, Sophia and I hadn't been able to raise him on the phone and we decided to go together to the flat. We were fearful of what we would find. And our fears were founded: my sweet, gentle and kind brother was dead.

He couldn't have been gone long; his body was still warm. But the paramedics who arrived within ten minutes confirmed his death and passed the responsibility for him to the police. Death is so strange. As I wept over the body of my dear brother, just three years older than me, my feelings were of overpowering sadness mixed with anger at Bob for dying so unnecessarily at the age of sixty-three. But there was also relief: relief that the hopelessness of his life was over and that he was at rest. Others would say such situations were never hopeless but having been heavily involved with his life for many years, including quite lengthy stays with me, I could see no way out, and, as his drinking increased, so did my concern for his future.

John and I had the awful job of giving our mother the terrible news, and the next day we drove down to her care home in Bexhill. My father had died the year before so he was spared the sorrow. There's no easy way of telling a mother that her son is dead, and it was made worse by her initial utter joy at our unexpected appearance. It came as a great shock as Bob's worsening condition had been kept from her. Somehow I think her faith and her advanced years (she was ninety-four at the time) helped her cope with it. She lived another two years and always had a photo of him with her.

I had an excellent relationship with my parents. I seemed to escape the temperamental teenage years, possibly because I was away at school so much of the time and relished rather than resented my time at home.

It was always special to return home from my various global forays to find an excited and warm welcome from them and we always enjoyed each other's company. However, they were not always there with the Welcome Home mat as they, too, did their fair share of travel abroad, particularly in America, which they got to know well. Their love affair with the States started in the early sixties with a three-month pulpit exchange with a church in Berkeley, California. Then, a few years later, an unexpected invitation arrived for my father from the British Council of Christian Churches for him to be one of a dozen British ministers on an exchange programme with American ministers. They all preached at a different church each Sunday, my papa's patch stretching from Florida to New England. He travelled by Greyhound bus from place to place and enjoyed wonderful hospitality staying in various family homes.

His Greyhound ticket – ninety days for $99 – then took him across the country to Vancouver where I was then living and where my mother joined him, having opted for a quicker route to Canada's west coast. Without his own church at that time, they decided to tarry a while in the States if they could find a temporary pastorate. Grass did not grow under their feet and soon they were on their way to another new experience, thanks to a response from a letter he wrote to the American Council of Churches enquiring about any empty pulpits 'anywhere in America'. Up came Silver City, a small town in New Mexico, once an Apache campsite.

My parents loved it, as indeed the Silver Cityites loved them. Sixties small-town America suited them well: they made some good and lasting friendships there and Mama found a new and absorbing hobby in the rocks, minerals and gemstones found in New Mexico. She became an avid collector of raw amethyst, quartz, opal, turquoise and lesser-known gems. If they didn't have a family to consider, they may well have stayed on longer than the nine months they allowed themselves. Their travels across the Pond weren't yet over as out of the blue came an invitation to return to the Berkeley church for a few weeks while they searched for a new and full-time incumbent.

My preacher man papa was in his seventies before he retired from his last church and continued Sunday preaching by request into his eighties. My parents' lives were never dull.

My father carried his ninety-two years brilliantly and his decline was sudden, following an infection he contracted during his one and only brief stay in hospital. I was with him on the day before he died and, as I was still living in London, stayed overnight with a friend who lived midway between London and Bexhill so I could get back to him relatively quickly the next day. I was about to leave for the forty-mile journey at 6 a.m. when the matron rang to say he didn't have long.

I exceeded all speed limits on that dash to Bexhill.

There was little traffic as, appropriately, it was a Sunday and the most beautiful spring day. When I arrived, my beloved papa was still alive, but I had just ten precious minutes with him before he slipped away. He appeared unconscious but I knew he could hear me.

After he'd gone, I remarked to the matron how lucky I was to have got there in time.

'He was waiting for you,' she replied. 'His expression changed when you walked in the door.'

Daddy's little girl.

My mother had gone into denial and had resolutely stayed in her bed next to him, so I found myself holding his hand and hers as he departed the world. It was very special for me to be with him when he died, just as it was for my mother's death three years later. She was ninety-six and in reasonable health for her age. A few hours after I'd been with her, she had a stroke and it was obvious she didn't have long to live. John and I experienced a strange phenomenon at her bedside. We were both holding her hands and, although seemingly unconscious, she knew we were there and, extraordinarily, with a vice-like grip took each of our hands in turn and put our fingers in her mouth. It was such an intimate and wonderful thing to do as she took her leave of her beloved family.

I cherish their memories.

The only immediate blood relation left in my generation is John, four years my senior, who has always played the big brother and been there for me. We're different characters entirely, but he's special and I love being with him and enjoy our nostalgic chats. He and his wife Jane live in East Grinstead, close enough for us to see each other quite often. I have stepchildren, Simon and Carol, but none of my own so my nephews and nieces – John's and Bob's children – have always been very important to me.

***

My London house went under offer and I was a couple of days from exchange on a house in Hove when the owner inexplicably pulled out, as the crazy property laws in England allowed her to do. I needed to act fast as I had my Burmese, Siamese and Abyssinian cats in tow. After a fruitless search for a temporary place to rent – three cats put the kibosh on that idea – I snapped up the next house I saw in Hove, a sizeable Victorian semi, after a brief look around, but I had clocked it needed a fair bit of work. I didn't see it again until I owned it.

After my speedy viewing, I was nervous at what I would find. On completion day, Lindsay and I drove down from London with a feline orchestra in the back of the car. It was a bleak December day in 1998, and I was anxious to have Lindsay's reaction to my impetuous buy – would it be oohs and ahhs and 'What a great buy' or 'Hmm, well, never mind, you can't win them all'? And I needed my poor put-upon friend with her Marigolds, as she's never happier than when elbow deep in those yellow rubber gloves.

We arrived to find yesterday's owners still in the house, making a half-hearted and totally unsuccessful attempt to clean it up. They seemed oblivious of the fact that this was no longer their house, but we shooed them on their way and were grateful for the Marigolds. Two pairs. And spares. As well as a family home for four, it had been a rooming house and behind every door lay a fresh horror. The common denominator was the stench. In each room there was a disgusting cooking stove which must have been used exclusively for fry-ups, judging from the stinking carpets soaked in congealed fat. And other indescribable odours. Every few minutes the ancient boiler would announce its presence with a long screech and the room filled with steam. The walls were black with condensation built up over many years. The garden was covered with paving stones, the only greenery being a single rosemary bush. But the house still got a big tick from us both, its potential being enormous.

The builders moved in almost immediately and did a brilliant job transforming it into a lovely home where I could enjoy my retirement. My days as a lady of leisure passed pleasantly enough with travelling, theatre going, devouring biographies, lunching with friends, creating collages, dog walking for The Cinnamon Trust and inspecting potential cat owners for Cats Protection.

It was what I'd always hoped my retirement would be, but it might have lost its charm before too long.

PART THREE

CHAPTER 21

CHARITY BEGINS 5,000 MILES AWAY

by Sylvia

As it happened, my new lady-who-lunches regime was short-lived. We all dread those middle-of-the-night phone calls as they can only be the bearer of bad news. As mine was on 4 December 2003.

Down a crackling line came a difficult-to-understand Indian voice. 'Hello? I am brother of Venkat.'

'Yes, hello?' I replied, tremulous in fear of bad news.

And then he just blurted it out. 'Venkat is dead. He killed in road accident.'

My mind went numb. Then, as I began to take on board this terrible news, my sobs joined his and we cried together down 5,000 miles of telephone line.

Fifteen years earlier in 1989, I'd made the offer to pay for Venkat's education. He'd said nothing at the time but I'd written my address on a scrap of paper and asked him to let me have his decision. Back home in England, I found myself thinking about him. Would he accept or would his father need him for fishing duties? Perhaps the idea of continuing his education and going to university was scary and he'd rather stay in the world that he knew.

I thought Venkat was a gutsy boy and hoped he'd be glad of the opportunity to get a good education. I'd taken a shine to him and felt in my bones that given the chance he could go far. I needn't have worried. Soon after my return, I came back from work to find an airmail letter on my door mat.

Yes please, he wrote. *This is big opportunity for me and I am happy. I will work hard. I will get degree.*

We kept in touch initially by snail mail and later by email. I saw him a couple of times. In fact, I was unexpectedly back in Kovalam the following year. There had been no chance to tell him so I asked some boys on the beach if they knew where he was.

'He's playing football,' they said. 'We go tell him you here.'

They took me to his home to wait for him – this had not been on our guided tour the year before. It was gloomy and dark and had no furniture except for an ancient mattress and a couple of floor mats. There was nothing on the crumbling walls – except for a photo of me! He had asked me to send it but I had no idea it was going to adorn a wall. I didn't have to wait long before Venkat came rushing in, happy to see me, as I was happy to see him.

Venkat loved his studies, did well and on to university he went. As promised, I continued to pay his fees. Twelve years after our first chance meeting and against all the odds, he graduated from Madras University with a Bachelor of Commerce degree. There was much rejoicing in the Venkat family, as indeed there was 5,000 miles away when the news reached me when I opened an airmail envelope to see a picture of Venkat at his graduation ceremony.

I nearly burst with pride.

He was keen to build a new house for his parents, their already ramshackle house having been half destroyed in a monsoon. The best money to be had was in Qatar and he secured a job in the hospitality industry, learning by experience in various hotel departments. In this way, he was able to save money for the family's new house. He also took it upon himself to learn Italian and became so proficient that he was able to supplement his hotel salary with translation work.

When the smart new house was built – this one with two bedrooms, running water and a bathroom – he returned to Kovalam. He emailed me excitedly to tell me that he'd been shortlisted for a job in Mumbai. That was the last time I ever heard from Venkat.

I was later to learn that the recklessness of youth and the call of adventure cost Venkat his life. He hadn't passed the driving test for 'two-wheelers,' the small motorbikes favoured by Indians and had little experience to do so. Big brother Janakiraman had refused to let him drive his bike but the ever-ingenious Venkat started the ignition with a pair of scissors, and off he went on the open road with heartbreaking consequences.

It was hard to believe that the boy whose progress I had proudly watched since my chance meeting with him on the beach fifteen years before would never realise his full potential or experience the joy of raising a family. He was just twenty-seven. His death hit me hard and although I'd seen little of him over the years, we were in touch regularly.

In a way he'd become my surrogate son.

Little did I know it then, but that dreadful phone call was to change my life for the rest of my days. I felt compelled to go back to Kovalam and had arranged for Janakiraman, the brother who had phoned me with the terrible news, to meet me at the hotel. He was two years older than Venkat, gauche and rather nervous (almost impossible to imagine today), but anxious to help in any way he could in his beloved brother's name. As I found the name Janakiraman too much of a mouthful, I said I would call him JR. The name stuck. He loves it.

He took me to see his family, by then living in the house that Venkat built. I have an abiding memory of his poor heartbroken parents, tears pouring down his mother's cheeks, which she mopped up with her saree. They spoke not a word of English, but we said a prayer together in front of the shrine in Venkat's memory. Rather touchingly, it included Jesus with the Hindu gods.

'I'd like to buy something for the village in Venkat's memory,' I said to JR. 'I thought maybe a television for the villagers to watch?'

I'd expected a warm response but I didn't get one.

'I don't think so,' was his unexpected reply.

He had other – bigger – plans. Like his brother, JR was as sharp as a whip, and the next day he steered me to Panchayat Union Primary School, known to all as PUPS, the only free school in the village.

I was horrified. It was dilapidated, there wasn't a stick of furniture in the place and just three unqualified teachers. The children were bedraggled, there was no energy and morale was palpably low. The headmistress was depressed about the lack of maintenance and teaching aids. She produced a wish list to improve the educational facilities in the village, ranging from blackboards for the primary school to a lock, stock and barrel high school, the village still being without any free education after primary age.

'Please help me,' she said.

Anyone who has the sense not to react impulsively

to such a request would have assured her that they would see what they could do and possibly do a whip round for the money for a blackboard. But not yours truly, who has always flown by the seat of her pants and allows her heart to speak before her head has a chance to get a look-in.

'Of course I'll help you,' I heard myself say. 'We can get the primary school sorted and then perhaps look at a high school for the village.'

I hasten to say this was not a magnanimous gesture on my part, just an over-the-top and ridiculous reaction to something that needed to be done. Foolhardy. Or perhaps plain stupid.

What had I done?

CHAPTER 22
KOVALAM

by Lindsay

Kovalam, or Covelong, is a traditional village on the south easterly corner of India, some twenty miles south of Chennai, the huge sprawling capital of Tamil Nadu. It is situated on a narrow spit of land between Chennai and the former French colonial settlement of Pondicherry, now Pudicherry, known locally as Pondi, on the Coromandel Coast, bordering the Bay of Bengal. To describe somewhere with a population of 8,000 and growing as a village seems odd to people in the west, for whom the word conjures up images of a church, pub and a cluster of houses. Kovalam feels small but at the same time, large.

Kovalam is, and always has been, a village of fishermen, dependent on the sea to sustain themselves and their families. Every evening when the weather allows, they take to the water in their small boats to fish by moonlight or a powerful lamp, returning at dawn with their catch. It's perilous work and accidents, some fatal, happen regularly. Those badly injured in a fishing accident are often left unable to work. No work means no money.

The village has grown up inland from the sea into a complex maze of alleys and brightly painted houses sitting cheek by jowl with leaf shacks, shops, temples and mosques. Most fishing families are Hindu, but significant Muslim and

Christian communities coexist harmoniously most of the time.

The main road through the village leads to the East Coast Road, which connects Chennai with Kanyakumari in India's far south. Cars, buses, lorries, motorcycles and tuk-tuks hurtle up and down with scant attention to speed restrictions and general rules of the road. There's always a sense of taking your life in your hands when crossing the ECR.

When Sylvia first visited Kovalam, many of the houses were made of palm leaf, which gave little protection from the elements and had to be replaced after each monsoon or cyclone. There's been a lot of building since and most – but not all – people have a more solid but still very modest house. They need it, as Kovalam has always had to endure appalling floods, cyclones, droughts and sea erosion.

Nowadays, a typical Kovalam house is made of bricks or concrete and consists of a couple of sparsely furnished rooms where families relax, study, eat and sleep. Hindu homes, however small, have a small shrine. Beds are not the norm, as most people sleep on a mat on the floor. Some families still cook outside on an open fire but increasingly there is a small basic kitchen with one or more gas burners. Thankfully kerosene is used less than previously, following a notable and fatal accident with an overturned kerosene stove, when a mother died leaving her two young children orphaned.

Many houses still have no bathroom. Water is collected from the pumps around the village and people either use the communal wash houses or the beach. In the mornings you can see mothers plaiting their daughters' hair, washing clothes in the village tanks or at the well and sweeping the front of their homes before creating a *rangoli*. These are patterns, often highly decorative and intricate, created on the ground with rice powder, white or coloured chalks or sand to bring good fortune or for celebration.

Incongruous though it may sound, the beating heart of the village, where the two main roads cross, is known as the Bus Stop. It's also an actual bus stop, where what seems like hundreds of local and long-distance buses pick up and drop off people going to and from work and school. Tuk-tuks zigzag between buses, cars and scooters carrying whole families, while pedestrians, ducks, cows, cats and dogs pick their way to safety. Stalls sell everything from jasmine garlands, fruit and vegetables to stationery, snacks, sarees, *lunghis* (men's clothing) and underpants. Men gossip at the twenty-four-hour tea booths and pilgrims pass on their way to visit the shrine of a famous Muslim saint who was a companion of the Prophet Mohammed himself.

It's a place of constant movement, noise and dust, which appears chaotic to the outsider but works to its own rhythm and rules.

Lining the streets around the Bus Stop are shops selling the necessities of life – meat, fish, vegetables, fruit and bread – alongside clothes, mobile phones, hardware, water, building materials and pawn shops. More recently some beauty salons, hairdressers and little supermarkets have sprung up.

Kovalam's people are delightful. Despite the hardship they have endured all their lives, they possess great dignity and style, and they laugh easily. No nuclear families for them: parents, children, grandparents, aunts and uncles all live together, often in one small room, and look after each other. Unlike in the big Indian conurbations, there are no orphaned children surviving on their own. Everyone has a roof over their head, albeit one that may leak.

The dawn chorus has none of the gentility of an English morning. The crows and cockerels shatter the peace of the night with a cacophony of cawing and crowing. As the fishermen unload their night's catch, cows, goats, dogs and people head for the beach. Chennai workers converge on the Bus Stop, the muezzin calls the faithful to prayer, the alleys and passages of Kovalam come alive and the sun climbs steadily up the sky for another scorcher of a day.

For all its poverty, Kovalam is a living example of a vibrant community.

CHAPTER 23

LIFE BEGINS (AGAIN) AT SIXTY-FIVE

by Sylvia

Back in the UK after my trip to meet JR and the rest of Venkat's family, I had serious second thoughts about my careless talk with the PUPS headmistress. What was I thinking, offering help to improve and provide education for the children of a poor Indian fishing village thousands of miles away? I could run a PR company in London standing on my head, but this was another ball game altogether, one I knew nothing about. And I'd retired, it was me time now.

I didn't have cold feet; they were blocks of ice. What had I done? I'd taken on a challenge I wasn't at all sure I could deliver. The makeover of the primary school wasn't too daunting, despite not having a clue how I could raise the funds, but given a fair wind I could have a shot at it and then perhaps give my excuses and opt out, back to my life of leisure in Hove.

I rebuked myself for not thinking things through before committing to ventures I knew nothing about. But I knew there was no going back, no halfway house. The die was cast. Resigned to my fate, I went to see a solicitor to set up the Venkatraman Memorial Trust.

Without preamble, I explained what the Trust would be about. There was no free education for the children of

Kovalam apart from a virtually derelict primary school with no professional teachers. I told him I planned to improve the facilities at that school and then build a much larger free high school for the twelve-to-eighteen-year-olds.

'My mission,' I said, 'is to see that no child in the village is denied education through an inability to pay the fees.'

He looked at me incredulously. 'You're sixty-five, newly retired and you're setting up an education charity in India?'

'Yes.'

'Have you worked in India before?'

'No.'

'Do you have experience in education?'

'No.'

'Have you worked in the charity sector before?'

'Never.'

When his eyes came down from looking heavenwards, he dutifully did the paperwork and the Venkatraman Memorial Trust came into being.

And suddenly I was excited about the adventure ahead. I wasn't cut out to be a lady of leisure and getting my teeth into such an unexpected and unusual project would be challenging but fun.

On that day in January 2004 at the Panchayat Union Primary School, my fate had been sealed, as unwittingly, had JR's. It was to be the best decision of my life.

The priority was to find someone to take on the India end, while I set up the UK operation and brought in the money.

The obvious thing would have been to seek out an important local person – a pillar of the Chennai community

– who knew everything about education, charities and the labyrinthine ways of the Indian government.

Instead I decided to take a gamble and ask JR to be the managing trustee. I had a hunch that I'd be backing a winner in this rather gauche young man.

JR couldn't run the Trust on his own and needed a fellow trustee to help. Again, I went for the least obvious choice: Ali, who had been one of Venkat's twelve-year-old friends at the prawns and fish café on the day I met Venkat fifteen years ago.

As it turned out, I'd backed not one winner but two.

CHAPTER 24

BRINGING IN THE BEANS

by Lindsay

With over 170,000 charities vying for funds in England and Wales alone, it was by no means a given that the money for the fledgling Venkat Trust would roll in. But as a newbie charity founder, Sylvia didn't know the rules of the game, what to do or how to do it. One thing was sure: she was going to do things her way and use all the tools at her disposal to make things happen. PR was always going to be part of the mix.

The Venkatraman Memorial Trust, known as the Venkat Trust, came into being on 24 May 2004. No time for any more cold feet. A circular to friends and contacts brought in just over £3,000, enough money to get things moving at PUPS. Once the Trust had been set up, we lost no time in cranking up the PR machine we knew so well to raise funds. The publicity we achieved brought in lots of supporters, most of whom have remained loyal to us to this day. JR and Ali had fun knocking down the worst of the crumbling buildings and supervising the construction of a two-storey classroom block and a dining hall with open side, which had been cleverly designed by Duncan Heather, Hampton Court garden designer and erstwhile client of the Emp to fit around a well in the limited space, otherwise unusable. He and his wife Carol were the first trustees.

Desks and benches arrived on a bullock cart, books were bought and qualified teachers appointed. PE went on the curriculum. As a *quid pro quo*, the Tamil Nadu government agreed to build two more classrooms on existing primary school land. A promising start in the relationship with the government, which was to have its ups and downs.

By the time PUPS was completed, it had become a school buzzing with happy, motivated children in smart new uniforms, provided by the Trust, enjoying their lessons and playtime with their friends.

Having been at the bottom of the pile, the school became a place parents wanted their children to go to and even won a first prize among fifty schools in the area for academic results, attendance and maintenance. The previously woeful literacy rates leapt from 60% to 95%. JR and Ali, who had little knowledge of bricks and mortar, became past masters of the building trade and supervised this and the many subsequent buildings that have gone up.

Playing to Sylvia and JR's predilection for property, land was bought opposite the school for a new building: the Venkat Tuition Centre. JR and Ali honed their newfound skills further on the two-storey building, which had a range of uses, not least offices for the Trust, an overflow for PUPS and a meeting place for the sponsored children, leaving plenty of outside space for a play area for the smaller children with swings and seesaws.

With such a positive story to tell, it wasn't difficult to interest *The Mail on Sunday*'s *You* magazine in running a feature by about the six-month-old charity covering Sylvia's chance meeting with Venkat, his subsequent tragic death and the setting up and progress of the Trust in his name.

Journalist Adrianne Pielou went to Hove to interview

Sylvia and her excellent article, *About a Boy* appeared as a two-page spread in the week before Christmas 2004. The catastrophic Boxing Day Tsunami struck a week later and Sylvia feared that any donations which might have been coming in the direction of the Trust would, quite understandably, be diverted to Tsunami relief charities.

How glad she was to be proved wrong. Collecting Trust mail from Hove's Royal Mail sorting office, she hoped there might be one or two cheques. She was handed 120 letters! Unable to contain her curiosity, she sat in the car park and opened every single envelope. Out fell the cheques like confetti. The final tally was 288 responses, amounting to more than £11,000.

What a stamp of endorsement. And what has been particularly important is that so many of those 288 donors are still supporters today, including financier James Morton, our most generous and consistent supporter from Day One. Testimony to Sylvia's ability to bring people with her.

Over the years PR would prove to be a priceless tool and the many national press, magazine features and radio interviews would bring in many new Venkat Trust supporters.

CHAPTER 25
A HIGH SCHOOL FOR KOVALAM

by Sylvia

PUPS may have been swiftly ticked off the to-do list, but there was a much bigger fish to fry: a high school for hundreds of children was sorely needed.

As it stood, free education in the village stopped at the end of the primary school years. For a Kovalam twelve-year-old the choices were bleak: pay for a private school, travel many miles to the nearest free school or leave school altogether. Alas, parents often had to take the last option. With no serious education to fall back on, a life of menial ill-paid jobs awaited, thus perpetuating the poverty that generations before had endured.

Not surprisingly, I hadn't held out much hope of ticking off a high school on the PUPS' headmistress's wish list back in 2004. But on 23 January 2013 I found myself, choked with emotion, standing outside a stunning new two-storey building – the Kovalam Government High School. I attended the grand opening day, blinking back tears as the children filed in to sit cross-legged underneath the striped awning, followed by teachers and parents. The great and the good were arriving in their impressive official cars and the boys' marching band was beating the hell out of drums bigger than themselves. I had a pair of scissors in my hand, ready to do the cutting of the ribbon honours with a Tamil

Nadu educational luminary.

Me? Was I really about to open a high school for a thousand pupils in an Indian fishing village, 5,000 miles from my Sussex seaside home? It was surreal.

The building of the school was a joint venture between the Tamil Nadu Government and the Venkat Trust, and both parties had signed the agreement in 2009. It seemed like a heaven-made arrangement but hell was to have its say – we'd calculated that we could have it built and the pupils installed by the end of 2010, but we hadn't factored in the bureaucracy, which was to drive us – particularly me – to the edge.

The wheels kept grinding to a halt. No sooner had something been agreed between the chief, the assistant chief and the deputy chief, than there was a change of government. Back we went to square one and another round of rubber stamps by officious officials all wanting their fifteen minutes of fame. I went to the government offices on several occasions with JR to chivvy them up. The school's progress was recorded in a large ledger and I wouldn't have been surprised if a quill pen had appeared. The manilla files were tied up with string. As Chennai is at the cutting edge of IT and one of the four top tech cities in the country, it was somewhat ironic that Tamil Nadu's government was still living in the last century. As a woman I also appeared to be invisible at some of the meetings I went to, also very last century.

Three frustrating years later, we finally got the okay and the sound of a JCB rumbling onto the land was music to my ears. First came the charming Hindu ceremony of Bhuma Puja, the blessing of the earth to propitiate its good energy and to seek forgiveness for killing worms and other earth-dwelling creatures.

Nothing was straightforward about the project. Huge boulders were discovered not far from the surface and had to be dynamited, foundations had to be dug deeper because of the salt content in the earth and so it went, on and on.

The Kovalam Government High School made its mark immediately, not least because the first headmaster was one of Tamil Nadu's best. Mr Chandrasekar had the gift of appearing *laissez-faire*, but there were no flies on him. He ruled the school with an invisible rod of iron and earned great respect from his students. Unfortunately for us, he moved on to be a schools' inspector but he keeps in touch with us and still calls it 'our school'.

The school has gone from strength to strength academically, sports-wise, pastorally. We were anxious to be promoted to higher secondary school status, which would allow us to include Standards 11 and 12, the sixth form. We knew this would be another bureaucratic mountain to climb but climb we did and upgraded we were. We were confident that our new status would attract admissions but the actual number in the first year brought in a staggering 606 more children! The students love the school and its many facilities, as do the teachers. Yet another building was needed for twelve more classrooms and two more science labs. Luckily, we had the space without encroaching seriously on the sports ground.

Many of the new arrivals came from fee-paying schools, much to the relief of parents who could ill afford the cost and often found themselves in serious debt. We were anxious to spread our net wider as we were aware that in many villages education was scant, or unsatisfactory, as it once was in Kovalam. JR's promotional tour of the outlying villages resulted in hundreds of children from twelve villages signing up. Their school journeys would have been tricky but the gift of a second school bus has enabled us to make a daily circuitous school run to and from the villages.

Without the fifty-fifty partnership the Trust has with the Tamil Nadu Government, the school (if indeed it existed, which is unlikely) would be unrecognisable. Most government schools have to go it alone and the budget for education allows for only the most basic of facilities. The statistics are worrying: 65% of India's 1.4 billion population live in 640,000 villages, not an easy fix educationally, and 90,000 of them have no school at all. It's little wonder that poverty is perpetuated from generation to generation. Given the proof we now have that education sees an end to poverty, it's sad that millions will never be given the opportunity to meet their potential and their menial existence will continue into future generations.

Thanks to the Trust's supporters who always manage to dig ever further into their put-upon pockets, the school is able to offer facilities which often surpass those in private schools. The English language audio visual lab has made a dramatic difference to students' written and spoken English, and they enjoy a state-of-the-art science lab, a 6,000-book library, more teachers to ensure small classes and two school buses. The result, of course, is good academic results that open university doors and spark promising careers. Sport is equally important and our well-maintained sports ground includes cricket nets and a bowling machine for our cricket-mad boys *and* girls.

Snooker came about when a UK supporter offered to give the school his antique table. I confess to being dubious about it as few knew what snooker was (although the game was invented in India), but I felt on safe ground as it would be impossible to get it to the other side of the world. Or would it?

Courtesy of the World Professional Billiards and Snooker Association, the table travelled several of the seven seas to its new high school home. Boys and girls alike loved the game from the start and, under their excellent tutor, have brought back a fair bit of silverware from their state tournaments in Chennai and other cities. We've even got a second table now. Our two best players hit the jackpot when they were invited by Jason Ferguson, the Association's Chairman, to attend the Indian Open, contested by the world's top professionals. The boys had never been out of the state before but now they were to travel with Ali to Visakhapatnam in Andhra Pradesh. It was a thrilling experience for them, and the icing on the cake was meeting the Open winner, John Higgins, who presented them with his cue chalk and bow tie. They're in a glass case in the school's snooker room. Three of our snooker boys now have excellent careers, either teaching at private clubs in Chennai or refereeing at major tournaments.

The school's flat roof has been transformed into a delightful garden, which the students love as an enjoyable break from their classrooms. They also have gardening lessons there, learning about India's indigenous flowers, how to grow vegetables for their families' cooking pots and the use of plants for medicinal use, much favoured by Indians. The garden features an arched walkway of flowers, a place for the vegetables and medicinal plants and a cool, shady sitting out area. It was built in memory of actress Gwyneth Powell, particularly known for her role as Mrs McClusky, the headmistress in the long-running BBC series, *Grange*

Hill. She was a wonderful supporter of the Trust in many ways as both a sponsor and visitor to Kovalam. Our most popular video features her splendid voice-over.

CHAPTER 26
CHANGE A CHILD'S LIFE

by Lindsay

I became a trustee soon after the Trust came into being and in one stroke, Sylvia and I were back to the Emp's glory days bringing all our PR skills into play to whip up publicity, build up supporters and devise ways to raise funds. Best of all, we could travel again, this time to India where the real work was happening.

The sponsorship scheme was launched in 2005 and was soon established as one of the Trust's most worthwhile activities. With the primary school purring along, Sylvia turned her attention to the children's welfare and she and JR put together a scheme whereby a modest regular cash injection would make a huge difference to the lives of Kovalam's poorest families.

It made perfect sense. After all, Sylvia's original sponsorship of Venkat was the reason behind everything. The education not usually available to poor families had been a life-changing experience for him.

Education is indeed life-changing, but the transformation doesn't happen overnight. Sponsorship, on the other hand, has an immediate effect and the moment a child is sponsored and the regular monthly payments arrive, they and their families experience a huge improvement in their lives. Like so many of the 665,000 villages in India, Kovalam is a village of have-nots and have-nots, with many families existing on a wage of £2 a day. Having a sponsor who pays the equivalent of a small takeaway coffee every week is a real game changer.

Quite a number of international charities run sponsorship schemes and I've signed up to a few over the years but, once matched with a child – or indeed, a grandparent – that was where the relationship finished and my monthly contributions disappointingly disappeared into a pot. I realise the reason is probably to do with safeguarding and the need to protect the child (or grandparent) but it's not insuperable. The Venkat Trust has been able to create a scheme where sponsor and child remain in regular touch through letters and cards, with all communications filtered through the Trust. No direct contact details are shared. Quite a number of sponsors have visited Kovalam and have met 'their' child and his or her family. It is a hugely fulfilling relationship on both sides.

Things started slowly. The Trust's very first sponsored child was eleven-year-old Sumithra, whose fisherman father had been killed in the Boxing Day Tsunami of 2004. Some years later, by now grown up and in a good job, she tearfully told Sylvia and me the tragic story of how, having lost her father, the only breadwinner, as well as her home, the penniless family was reduced to begging for scraps just to survive. The trauma will never leave her but sponsorship changed her life. Without it, Sumithra would have left school at twelve to earn a few rupees a day to survive sweeping the streets or carrying bricks on her head on a building site. Instead, the security of sponsorship allowed her intelligence to flourish and, having graduated with her first degree, she was offered a place on a Master's course, after which she became an accountant. Her status changed and, as an educated woman, her arranged marriage was to a man with a good career and prospects.

More than 400 Kovalam children now have a sponsor in the UK, or elsewhere in the world. Some have been sponsored from their early days at PUPS and have been able to share their progress through school and on to university with their sponsor in their cards and letters. The neediest children are identified by Ali, who knows the village and everyone in it, and he and Aarthi work together with Sylvia's niece Emma in the UK to match them with a sponsor.

I remember visiting Udayakumar's house to catch up with one of the earliest sponsored children. He was an only child whose father died in a fight before he was born and whose mother earned a few rupees a week in a Chennai sweatshop making leather jackets for the luxury market in Dubai. On the wall of their simple home was a photograph of his sponsoring family, a typical shot of mum, dad and kids in an English garden. And there in the middle was Udayakumar. He had cut out a photo of himself and added it to the group. There were a few misty eyes when his sponsors heard this. Thanks to them, the clever boy was able to go to university and, as a qualified and well-paid mechanical engineer, his and his mother's lives are now transformed. At last she has been able to give up her job in the Chennai sweatshop.

With the numbers of sponsored children ever increasing, the Venkat Tuition Centre was bulging at the seams by 2016 and the Trust too needed more office space. Happily, we had bought land in the early days to provide a sports ground for PUPS and there was land to spare for yet another edifice. A very large edifice: the ground floor being one enormous room, bigger than a tennis court with no pillars. The Janakiraman Community Hall, the JR Hall, named in recognition of JR's extraordinary contribution to the success of the Venkat Trust, provides ample space for the 400 sponsored children's various Sunday morning activities and is an ideal place for concerts and the like. It's also an ideal refuge for villagers during floods and cyclones when their houses become uninhabitable. The upstairs space with moveable partitions appears to have elastic walls as it provides spacious Trust offices, a small library, the University Club social room, a large model railway for the younger children and our crowning glory: the immensely successful English language audio/visual lab. Nearby Chennai is a huge centre of the global IT industry and also the health capital of India with many career opportunities for well-qualified young people, but fluent English is essential. Thanks to the language lab, both written and spoken English have improved beyond recognition.

Sponsorship isn't a free meal ticket. Once sponsored, a child must attend school regularly, work hard and become part of the Trust community, joining in the weekly activities in the JR Hall which include chess, tapestry, art, music, letter writing and English stories. The uni students are generally glad to show their appreciation for the opportunities they've been given and willingly attend the Sunday morning get-togethers, each taking charge of one of the groups of younger children. They also love bossing everyone about at the hugely popular annual Trust sports days. There have even been donations to our work from some former sponsored children who have gone on to well-paid jobs and want to share their good fortune.

The Trust provides important pastoral care, helping

children and young people to cope with bereavement (it being all too common to lose a parent in their childhood) and any family or school concerns they may have. When the time comes to think about the future the Trust helps them find the best route – academic or vocational – and then to choose the right course. An inordinate amount of care is given to each individual child. Sylvia describes sponsorship as a child being 'taken under the wing of the Venkat Trust', and this is the perfect description of the relationship.

At any one time there are about seventy-five sponsored young people at university. As well as their fees being paid, they have access to the University Club in the JR Hall, which arranges social and cultural activities to help with their transition from village to business life. They can also use the language lab to bring their English up to the level they will need for work.

'I cannot think of a better investment than sponsoring a child, and to have the satisfaction of seeing his or her life turned around and appalling deprivation made a thing of the past,' Sylvia often says.

She's right. It's a win-win situation: the sponsors themselves are beneficiaries as they bond with their children as they progress through school and, in most cases, university.

Of course, not all the children are academically inclined, but they can choose and train for vocational careers such as beauticians, tailors, mechanics and electricians with scope for satisfying, well-paid jobs.

The majority of the sponsored children are Higher Secondary School pupils and many have illiterate or semi-illiterate parents. This might suggest that they fall behind their better-off friends academically, but this is not the case. They are every bit as bright as their peers and many excel both academically and in sport.

Sisters Yuvarani and Kaviya were sponsored fourteen years ago when they were just eight and six years old. Now both graduates, Yuvarani has a coveted job with Tata Consultancy Services, the IT company within the mega international conglomerate, and Kaviya has an equally prestigious job. It would take their odd-job-man father fifteen years to earn what Yuvarani will earn in a year. The family has just moved into a new house paid for by the sisters.

If anything, we tend to have more sponsored girls than boys, and thankfully gender doesn't hold back girls progressing in professional careers in South India. I'm not sure I could be so confident about the north. We have many girls who have graduated and are prospering through their careers in IT, medicine, law, banking, computer engineering and the civil service, and continue to work once they marry and have children.

If anyone needed to be persuaded that their sponsorship is not just money well spent but life-changing, the story of sisters Shipana and Sulaykha Banu proves the point. Aged just five and three, they were living in Chennai when their parents were killed in the Tsunami. A peripatetic, poverty-stricken life with various relatives then followed for the little orphans until they made their way to Kovalam with an older sister and enrolled at the high school.

The headmaster spotted their exceptional ability and, aware of their tragic circumstances, asked the Trust to find sponsors. We also helped them with a suitable place to stay and, when the time came, to choose their university courses. Shipana is now a highly qualified hospital technician and scrub nurse and Sulaykha Banu a lawyer.

The boys do well too. Kather Mytheen's family came to Kovalam on a pilgrimage when he was still a small boy and stayed as his father became ill. We've known him since primary school when he stood out from the others with his charm and confidence, and he has always been happy to help with anything the Trust needs. Kather's family's sole income came from his father selling handkerchiefs on the pavement and they lived in one room with no running water or sanitary facilities. With his sponsor's help and the Trust's support he gained a first-class degree in computer engineering and is now progressing fast up the career ladder. He has moved his family to a two-bedroom house with all mod cons and set his father up with a thriving shop selling menswear.

Had he not been a sponsored child, tall, dark and handsome Muthumani could never have dreamed of taking up the offer of a coveted place at Amet, one of India's most prestigious naval colleges. This fisherman's son is now an officer in the Indian Merchant Navy and on the way up. Other particularly high achievers are on course to become a neurosurgeon, an Artificial Intelligence specialist and a clinical psychologist.

CHAPTER 27
IT'S A PEOPLE THING

by Lindsay

JR and Sylvia are an unusual partnership. As chance would have it, they were both born on 6 December, albeit thirty-five years apart. On one hand they have nothing in common – culture, language or background – but on the other, they are soulmates.

Like Sylvia, JR is possessed of a presence, which means people take notice when he speaks and he's who people go to when they're in trouble or there's some problem in the village. A committed Hindu, he observes all the religious traditions and festivals. Sylvia may tick Christian on forms and be word perfect in an impressive number of hymns, but that's a hangover from her church upbringing.

Critically, they both share a sense of humour. JR's laugh is a joy to hear. There is always a lot of laughing when Sylvia and JR are together in Kovalam.

When he and Sylvia met, he was still a bachelor and had already started to flex his business muscles. They share the same entrepreneurial urge. He set up a prawn hatchery in Andra Pradesh, the next state to Tamil Nadu and, more locally, a gym in Kelambakkam, Kovalam's much larger neighbour. They both share a fascination with property development, which has proved such a boon when securing land for Trust buildings, as well as planning and project managing the actual construction.

He loves his village and is inordinately proud of it and its inhabitants. A big fish in a small pond, perhaps, but JR has never wanted to live anywhere else. When he married Uma in 2005, he moved from his parents' house to a new build in the heart of the village, close to the ever-buzzing Bus Stop. Daughter, Thanuja, was born the next year, followed a few years later by son, Balaji. Family is everything to JR and he adores his children, who have grown into confident and charming young people, fluent in English, westernised on one hand but very Indian on the other. Proud of who they are and where they live. A credit to their parents.

JR is a natural politician, intuitively able to navigate the arcane intricacies of local and state politics. On a local level, villages are run by the Panchayat, which devolves state government to the villages and come under the overall control of a president. It is a hugely important and influential job, with responsibility for every aspect of village life, from planning to education, as well as sorting out disputes, which can flare up at any time in a society still defined by caste and religion.

Aged just thirty-two in 2007, JR decided to wade into this political minefield and run for president of Kovalam. Despite his relative youth, he was already a well-known person around the village, particularly for his work for the Venkat Trust, but securing the majority vote was to take weeks of rallies, speeches and promises to win over the voters.

Sylvia happened to be in the village as campaigning was reaching its climax, and found herself addressing a huge crowd gathered at the Bus Stop – with simultaneous translation into Tamil – on why JR was the man for president. It must have helped, as a few weeks later he emerged victorious from the hard-won battle and able to make the difference to his beloved village he'd been longing to make. Now he had the power and he determined to use it wisely.

JR went on to serve two five-year terms as president of Kovalam and during those ten years, together with the Venkat Trust, he was able to transform the educational landscape of his village, using his skills, contacts and access to power to make sure the necessary orders were secured and work was carried out properly and accountably.

Tamil Nadu, like the rest of India, is run according to the structures and processes of the Raj. Sylvia had to learn about District Collectors, Public Works Departments, District Rural Development Officers and the like, as these were the people who would control all the big decisions. Feet-dragging comes with the territory and interdepartmental squabbles and politicking can hold things up by months, if not years. None of this played to Sylvia's patience, or lack thereof.

But together Sylvia and JR are a formidable team. They are both practical and pragmatic problem solvers.

'I do it,' is a great JRism, usually accompanied by 'One hundred percent'.

Each has a work ethic that makes things happen. Over the four years between securing the land for Kovalam Government High School and the first pupil arriving in 2013, Sylvia's twice-yearly visits to the village and every day in between were spent trying to break down bureaucratic barriers. Every time they hit a brick wall, JR would find another route through. It might involve persuading the rich and powerful of Tamil Nadu to put a word in the right ear, or doorstepping a state potentate until he – it was always a he – realised the Venkat Trust in the shape of Sylvia and JR wasn't going to go away. It was less painful to sign the order that was, for example, holding up the building of the desperately needed Kovalam Government High School, than to wallow in the pleasure of power.

There is huge respect on either side. Both have a clear sense of direction and a dogged determination to do what they've set out to do and to take people with them along the way. Each has his or her own methods for doing this. While JR understands how patiently to manoeuvre a path through the convoluted Tamil Nadu politics, Sylvia has less time for what she sees as petty bureaucracy. There's no shortage of the latter in India and she has spent many an hour being ignored by minor officials behind desks groaning with papers tied up in pink string while attempting with JR to navigate the latest official maze. Minor officials have learned that they ignore Sylvia at their peril. She is a mistress of the art of persuasion.

Neither suffers fools gladly but is at the same time the personification of kindness to people in genuine need. They share a common loathing of injustice. JR will always stick up for a villager who has made a mistake that could destroy hard-won prospects, and when Sylvia heard that JR had been barred from entering a three-star in Chennai because he was Indian, she protested, 'Barred from entering a hotel in *your own country*?' and had to be actively restrained from taking issue with the wretched place.

Meanwhile, Ali was a tearaway child from the Muslim end of Kovalam, who broke away from his family when he was ten years old. His mother died of rabies, sadly not an uncommon cause of death in village India, where stray dogs roam free. His fisherman father remarried, but far from giving the sad little boy the love and care he desperately needed, his new stepmother treated him badly and Ali's life soon became much worse.

Ali flies in the face of everything the Trust is about – he stopped going to school when he was ten and hasn't had any formal education since. He did actually attend every day, but just for lunch, his only meal of the day. He slept on the beach and, in his own words, 'roamed like a rowdy and no one respected me.'

Venkat and JR sorted him out. The two young Hindu brothers and the rowdy Muslim lad became the closest of friends.

While Ali's childhood trauma may have cost him his education, the well-worn 'university of life' cliché did him no harm. He can turn his hand to anything, from managing gangs of builders to photography or organising large parties with full catering. Once he and his father had put their differences behind them, Ali's impressive strength was a welcome addition to the crew in those days before motors, when the fishing boats had to be rowed out into the deep waters. He had a side hustle as one of a syndicate selling shells to foreign tourists at Fisherman's Cove Hotel, which was quite lucrative until the escalating room rates appealed only to business guests. To this day he has kept his pitch and a few times a month he takes his shells and pearls up to the posh end of the beach and sometimes strikes lucky.

When Sylvia returned to Kovalam after Venkat died, Ali was already married to Abebabi and his daughter Sumaya had been born. She and her younger sister Nafila are the joys of Ali's life. Having had only the scantest education himself, he has insisted theirs is the best it can be and Sumaya and Nafila have grown to be as clever as they are beautiful. They have become forthright young women with their own views on religion, politics and the world in general, but with the sensitivity to respect the mores of a traditional Indian village.

Kovalam may have a population of 8,000 but Ali knows every single one of them. He knows where they live, what they do, their children's names and any problems they may have. When the Trust introduced the sponsorship scheme, Ali was able to identify the children who would benefit most under its nurturing wing, as well having as some extra money each month.

The last piece in the jigsaw, Aarthi, arrived sometime later when the numbers of sponsored children continued to rise sharply and a professional administrator became essential. Her fluent English is invaluable when things get a bit lost in translation, and her organisational skills are a marvel. Slender, elegant, calm and super-efficient, Aarthi keeps on top of all the children's academic performances and is a listening ear for any problems they may have. When the exam results for the final school year (Standard 12) come in and children make their plans for the next stage of their education, Aarthi helps them through the mysteries of choosing which university to go to and what to study.

She maintains an iron grip on the ever-increasing paperwork demanded by the Indian government as it seeks to stamp out charity money laundering and keep alive the stereotype of the more paperwork the merrier. In recent years, hundreds of charities have been summarily closed down for supporting terrorism or proselytising. Every single penny spent has to be accounted for, which takes time and effort but means there are no loose ends.

Sylvia and I were the only UK trustees after Duncan and Carol Heather had to step down because of other commitments. We've carried on where we left off at the Emp, enjoying the challenge, the joy of being able to continue working together and loving our visits to Kovalam.

More recent trustees are Sarah Da Silva, and Nick Goslett who both live near Sylvia in Hove. Sarah is wonderful with people, an excellent sounding board, and takes on a range of different projects for the Trust, while former Deloitte director Nick helps with systems and is endlessly patient with Sylvia's frequent IT dramas. Both have visited Kovalam many times over the years.

The four of us are knocking on a bit and the arrival of John Whelan was a welcome injection of youth. Sylvia met him when he came to paint her house in Hove. While wielding his paintbrush in her office, he quizzed her on what she did at her desk every day and immediately volunteered to go out to Kovalam for a couple of weeks to smarten up some classrooms. It was his Road to Damascus moment. When he saw the poverty in the village, he said that he became a different man there and then and resolved to do everything possible to help the village. He has and he does, and when Sylvia asked him if he would like to be a trustee, he happily agreed. The Trust got two for the price of one, a kind of serendipitous BOGOF, as John's partner Alex fell in love with it too. As our honorary fundraiser, she has thrown her huge energy into spreading the word about our work through her successful fitness and friendship network to raise funds. Each year the members of her 'UberMummies' community raise thousands of pounds running the annual Brighton Half Marathon. John and Alex are a big asset and are regular visitors to Kovalam. Their friendliness and enthusiasm mean they know everyone in the village and all the sponsored children adore them. A further fresh injection of younger trustees has come in the form of Natalie Lee and Frankie Knight.

CHAPTER 28

TSUNAMI, FLOODS, CYCLONES AND COVID

by Sylvia

The Boxing Day Tsunami of 2004 struck just a few months after the Venkat Trust was set up. The world was in shock as we received the unbelievable news of the death of 225,000 people in fourteen countries and the appalling destruction. It was hard to comprehend and, of course, I was concerned about Kovalam, JR, Ali and all the children. Were they okay?

For hours I tried to contact JR but all lines of communication were down. Finally, after an agonising wait, he managed to get through to me from an inland village. While I was relieved to hear they were all safe, it was alarming that he already knew of ten deaths and the sea had shown no mercy with its destruction. Houses were flattened, fishing boats reduced to matchwood. Chennai, just twenty miles up the coast, suffered terribly when people poured onto the word's second longest beach to watch the sea behaving in such a strange way – with horrific consequences.

JR had been standing outside his parents' home on the beach when the Tsunami hit. He noticed the sea was receding into the far distance. He knew nothing about tsunamis but sensed danger. Indeed, the giant wave was already making its fateful journey back to Kovalam's beach

– and way beyond. He rushed into the house and flung his startled mother over his shoulder – luckily the only other occupant at that time – then climbed onto the roof, jumped onto the house behind and from there sprinted to safety with his precious cargo. His house was swamped by the wave but, being brick built, survived, as did the house next door, which was to become the UK trustees' home on their visits to Kovalam.

With one treacherous wave, the fishermen lost their boats and their livelihood. Their families lived a hand-to-mouth existence anyway and now they had no income at all. Something had to be done, and fast. The Venkat Trust was still in its infancy but we needed another charity so we could replace some of the smaller boats and get the fishermen back to sea. The Kovalam Tsunami Appeal was set up and registered with the Charity Commission and the same solicitor who was understandably concerned about my credentials for the Venkat Trust kindly gave his services free of charge.

The boats were called catamarans, a word that originated in Tamil Nadu. Unlike the usual two-hull meaning, the Indian *cat* is a single hull, skiff-type boat shaped from tree trunks and lashed together. The special wood grown in neighbouring Kerala was brought in by lorry and a boatyard was set up on the beach. Our generous supporters enabled us to build twenty-five boats and equip them with engines to get the fishermen back to work.

I went out to Kovalam myself to see how things were progressing and was struck by the camaraderie as the villagers helped each other to cope with the appalling disaster – the bereaved and homeless, the shattered village, demolished boats and loss of income. The Trust set up a free food and blankets base in the Tuition Centre, which was a lifeline for many.

All these years later and the effects of the Tsunami are still felt. The sea currents changed and fish stocks have been permanently reduced, an ever-worrying situation for the thousand-plus fishermen relying on the nightly catch for their livelihood.

It's always the poorest countries in the world that suffer the worst of the natural disasters. Why them and not the rich countries? Come on, God, if you *are* there, just give them a break. In my time, Kovalam has suffered from terrible flooding, drought, cyclones and sea erosion, which threatened the villagers' houses on the beach and the fishing. The sea suddenly took it upon itself to advance beyond the beach, finally receded and has stayed put since.

Along with most of the rest of the world, Kovalam was also affected by Covid. Only a handful of small island countries escaped its wrath. India was badly hit and in most parts there was a dire shortage of hospital beds, oxygen and vaccine. Social distancing and masks don't sit well with Indians even when, as in the case of Kovalam, one in ten adults had the disease. The generous response to our Covid appeal enabled JR and Ali, dressed in full PPE gear and looking as though they were about to take off for the moon, to distribute food parcels to the homes of thousands of needy people.

The Covid sufferers and their relations had been travelling on crowded buses to go to an equally crowded hospital in Kelambakkam in search of medication, spreading the infection like wildfire. We cut out the need for crowded travelling by attaching a makeshift large and shady waiting room to the village's tiny hospital. Its spaced-out seating and dispensaries for medicine resulted in a dramatic drop in the infection rate. This small, well-run hospital, which was built on the edge of the village while JR was President of Kovalam, was a lifesaver, often in the literal sense, and without it, Covid would have been catastrophic for the village.

Floods are bad enough anywhere in the world. In a place like Kovalam where some of the population still live in flimsy palm leaf houses, people can be left homeless as many homes collapse or are flooded. Fishing has to stop which means the fishermen's income stops too, and it is a precarious time for the village. The Trust helps out with food served from a lorry and supplies blankets where needed.

CHAPTER 29

HAPPY HOUR AT LAKSHMI HOUSE

by Lindsay

It's difficult to run a charity 5,000 miles away and time spent in Kovalam is invaluable. Sylvia goes two or three times a year with me or with one or more of the trustees and sometimes supporters too.

The London flight arrives in the small hours at Chennai Airport and as we emerge from the terminal into the wall of heat, JR appears from the teeming crowd to greet us. In the early days, it was a formal handshake; later he would submit reluctantly to an awkward embrace, arms clamped to his sides; but now it's a proper luvvie-style hug.

Thanagar, JR's driver, waits for us by the car and the drive to Kovalam takes just under an hour at that time and three times as long otherwise in the impenetrable traffic. We speed through the darkness as Tamil Nadu is waking up. Sleepy commuters make their way to their bus stop, hoping to find a seat on the bus and the chance to catch a few more minutes of sleep. Gaudily painted lorries on their long drive to the south overtake us, horns blaring. People gather at the tea kiosks for the first cup of the day and dogs and cows set off on their daily search for something to eat.

We drive through the waking streets of Kelambakkam, along the narrow road that crosses the Kovalam backwaters and glimpse the Higher Secondary School as it catches the first rays of the day. Then on, into the village. At last, the moment we've been longing for.

We're back!

Dawn is breaking as we reach Lakshmi House, the trustees' home in Kovalam where a beaming Ali greets us at the gate. The house backs onto one of the most exuberantly noisy Hindu temples in the village. It's loud at the best of times and emits twenty-four-hour top decibels during any of the many festivals celebrated in India.

Lakshmi House is a charming single-storey building, painted white and simple but very comfortable with two bedrooms and bathrooms, a kitchen and delightful sitting room and separate self-contained garden room. In the middle of the sitting room is a palm tree growing through the open-to-the-sky roof, recently joined by a fast-growing pawpaw, an uninvited but welcome and productive guest. It's a particular source of delight in the monsoon when the rain comes down in sheets, watched by the dry residents a few feet away.

Surrounding it is a beautiful garden filled with scented frangipani, hibiscus, jasmine, lilies and scrambling yellow trumpet flower. Tall coconut palms sway exotically and JR, a firm believer in the healing properties of plants, has been known to summon a man to shin to the top to collect fresh coconuts so Sylvia could be given a coconut milk cure for some malady. It's his go-to remedy for most ailments.

Lakshmi House sits on the beach with its terrace overlooking the Bay of Bengal, a glorious place to sit at any time of the day or night and catch the breeze off the sea. All along the beach, the colourful wooden boats line up ready for the night's fishing. There's always something going on. In the mornings the fishermen return, sort their catch and sell some of the prime specimens straight from the boat before a slow day repairing nets. The 1900 fishermen have the loudest voice in Kovalam and in recent years have sadly splintered into Hindus and Muslims. We hope that will change. The Hindus are by far the larger group with a fleet of 180 boats. JR's Hindu fisherman heritage goes back generations and his is a powerful voice in the often-quarrelsome group, using his skills of diplomacy to sort out disputes and solve problems.

The lagoons that spring up on the beach after the monsoon are full of fish, much to the delight of the pied kingfishers, which hover like helicopters waiting to dive when the slightest movement signals lunch. Elegant egrets, squat little herons and even the occasional painted stork find rich pickings in the surrounding shallows. Over a delicious lunch of fish from the night's catch cooked by one of Ali's relatives on an open fire, our entertainment includes watching the cavorting goats who patrol up and down the beach before being marshalled in single file by Boss Billy Goat and moved to pastures new. Cows amble contently and on hot days the dogs break off their endless play to cool down in the water. As the sun goes down bats emerge from their nests under the roof tiles and flit briefly in and out of the house before darkness falls.

Sylvia adores cats and Kovalam has plenty. On one visit we were adopted by the sweetest little tabby, a stray we tried to ignore but ended up feeding against our better judgment. She was thrilled to see us for obvious reasons and we succumbed. Now (Moaning) Minnie lives at Lakshmi House and Sylvia and I have set up a Minnie Food Fund. Prema, who looks after the garden, looks after her too.

Although not yet seen on the beach, there are monkeys in the village near the Bus Stop. They sit on walls and rooftops waiting for a chance to snap up a tasty morsel and generally don't stray too far.

But not always.

Sylvia had an uneasy breakfast with a monkey who came to call uninvited when she was in the house on her own. In the kitchen peeling a pawpaw, she was horrified when a large furry paw came into view and her breakfast disappeared. Monkeys can be intimidating, not just because of their size and nasty incisors but they are fearless, and this one fixed Sylvia with brazen look while it smugly tucked into the pawpaw.

'I was so relieved when he left,' she told me later. 'I immediately shut all the doors and windows – and then remembered that he could easily get through the open roof. A slightly unnerving experience!'

Games of football, cricket and kabaddi rage all over the beach whenever schools are out, and at weekends and on the incessant Indian public holidays, the beach throngs with people. They picnic, chat and swim, modestly attired. Some come from Kovalam but many are what JR and Ali refer to disapprovingly as 'Chennai People', to whom any bad behaviour can be attributed.

Sylvia tells me the short distance from Lakshmi House to the JR Hall is a commuter journey on a par with – if not better than – her previous more exotic journeys to work, including San Francisco's cable car and the Star Ferry across Hong Kong harbour. On cool mornings we sometimes walk through the streets, or JR or Ali will scoop us up to ride pillion but Sylvia's tuk-tuk, which she bought as her eightieth birthday present to herself, is now our chariot of choice. It is also a welcome source of extra money for Thanagar, who has the use of it as a weekend taxi.

We pass villagers going about their daily business, women sweeping their doorsteps and drawing a *rangoli*, cleaning their teeth with a twig, plaiting and ribboning their daughters' hair, having a good old chat or a row with neighbours and drawing water from the well. The fish market is always busy, the noisy fishwives swatting away the flies from their wares and spreading the latest gossip.

★★★

Happy Hour is one of our favourite times. After a busy day, JR and Ali join us in the evening for a glass of winebox wine from our luggage or duty-free brandy, JR's chosen tipple. Sylvia decorates the terrace with candles and lights and we settle down for a chat.

A subject of conversation we all enjoy is comparing Indian and British cultures. JR and Ali are always pleased to explain the mysteries of Indian culture and we can never hear enough.

Indians are more formal than the Brits and definitely more respectful of those older than themselves. We've tried to persuade Aarthi to call us by our first names – as JR and Ali do – but she says she just can't. It's always Sylvia Mam or Lindsay Mam, or just Mam. Indeed, one of the many highlights of Sylvia's eightieth birthday weekend was the ten-foot-high banner outside the JR Hall proclaiming *Happy Birthday Sylvia Mam*.

JR used to be very formal and careful about the subjects he would discuss with the female trustees. Now he's got our measure and anything goes topic wise. And there's a flip side – we're coy about subjects that the Indians have no problem in speaking about. Take menstruation, always the unmentionable, even at school when we would conceal sanitary towels under our tunics. Not so in India. When JR asked us to his daughter Thanuja's menstruation party, we thought he'd got the wrong English word. But no, it was a celebration of Thanuja's first period. This rite of passage into womanhood is celebrated only in South India and is actually a rather charming way of recognising the transition from girl to woman. Initially, Thanuja had to be on her own in a separate room for a day or two, which she didn't enjoy, but then a big party was held. She wore a saree for the first time in her life, sat in some splendour and her relatives brought her gifts of fruit and flowers. We were honoured to be invited.

While not in the same taboo league as menstruation, cystitis is hardly dinner party conversation. Sylvia had a bout of it in Kovalam and the ever-obliging JR went chasing around the state looking for cranberry juice – and triumphed. But it didn't cure the problem. She asked him to make an appointment for her to see the local doctor, not expecting a home consultation. In a trice, the doc arrived at Lakshmi House where trustees and friends were chatting. Did Sylvia manage to steer him to a corner and whisper the embarrassing symptoms to him? Not a chance. He sat down in the middle of the assembled company where the consultation took place with a fascinated and fully participating audience.

Kovalam is a good example of different faiths living harmoniously side by side. Hindus, Muslims and Christians get on well and enjoy each other's festivals and events. Everyone celebrates Christmas and Hindu festivals are fun for all. Perhaps the Muslims' special days don't have quite the same appeal; not many non-Muslims would choose to observe Ramadan, when no food or drink can be taken from the first light of dawn to the setting of the sun.

Hindus love their festivals, of which there appear to be hundreds, and scores of them come with national holidays. How does India ever get any work done? Diwali, the Festival of Lights, is celebrated throughout the world, and Tamil Nadu has its own big event, Pongal – what a splendid word – to celebrate Harvest Festival. It's a four-day extravaganza of feasting, gift-giving and visiting homes in January, and the music is incessant and ear-splitting and goes on into the night. Loudspeakers are set up all over the village and we have the misfortune at Lakshmi House to have a mega-decibel, tinny loudspeaker outside the temple opposite us. (Misfortune for our untuned ears, but loved by all the Kovalamites, who enjoy every minute of this joyful celebration). The animals are part of the festivities, too. Cows and goats have their horns brightly painted and beribboned. Even without Pongal, there's very little quiet in the village, as we're called to prayer by the muezzin regularly during the night, while the Catholic church relays its sermon by loudspeaker to us all early on Sunday mornings.

The Trust is strictly secular, although we're always amused at the Sunday morning gatherings of the sponsored children who start their activities with a rousing rendition of 'All Things Bright and Beautiful'.

Indian weddings fascinate us. Nearly all marriages in Kovalam are arranged and can happen any time from age sixteen onwards. It is very important for parents to secure a good marriage for their daughter, and saving gold for her dowry starts as soon as a baby girl is born. Often the couple have barely met and have sometimes not even been alone together. The ceremony reflects this, with the exquisitely dressed bride and groom looking terrified before being united by a holy man, while people mill around chatting. A feast of biryani follows, mercifully without alcohol (with it the cost of a wedding could ruin a family). Unfortunately, custom and family honour require that weddings are elaborate affairs, and people often have to borrow from loan sharks to cover the cost, putting themselves in hock forever.

The bride's house is decorated with flags and bunting and surrounded by super loud speakers belting out Bollywood favourites for what feels like twenty-four hours a day before everyone repairs to the marriage hall or temple, to be joined by hundreds of people, who all bring gifts for the couple.

On marriage, a girl must leave her home and village to live with her husband's family, whom she barely knows. There she starts a new life as a stranger in a new place, with a husband who is virtually a stranger himself. Traditionally, women become housewives after they get married and stay at home to care for the house and children, who arrive in short order. There are exceptions: the fish market is run by fearsome fishwives, but they are older and their children grown up. A woman will have to find work if widowed or abandoned by her husband, but this is usually as a street sweeper or on a building site, where the sight of women in sarees carrying loads of bricks on their heads is commonplace.

Education changes all of this, of course, and the arrival of the Venkat Trust has transformed the future of Kovalam's young women, enabling them to join the ranks of teachers, nurses, doctors, accountants, bankers, lawyers, psychologists and IT specialists.

CHAPTER 30
THE BIG BIRTHDAY BASH

by Sylvia

There were two events to celebrate in January 2019: the Venkat Trust was clocking up its fifteenth birthday and I had just had my eightieth birthday. Both difficult to believe.

It was time to celebrate and where better than in Kovalam? A weekend party was planned and the early hours of 24 January saw Lindsay, JR, Ali and me at Chennai Airport, awaiting the arrival of the British Airways flight from London. As well as the family and trustees – who had a three-line whip – I'd hoped that some friends and supporters would also make the long journey to South India. But I never expected such a good response: forty-six party seekers tumbled out of the airport into Chennai's early morning sunshine.

And what a party it was – a joyful experience from start to finish.

Visiting schools in an off-the-beaten-track Indian village is an interesting experience for anyone. To go to a flourishing high school which would not have existed without their and other supporters' donations has to be quite special.

The guests sat in on lessons, took part in science experiments, checked out the library's books, tried their potting skills at the snooker tables and showed off their batting ability – or otherwise – from a bowling machine in the cricket nets. They all fell in love with the PUPS' adorable youngsters, who put on a splendid gym display.

For their part, the sponsored children were beside themselves with excitement. Most of the UK group were sponsors and visited their children at their homes, watched their concert of singing and dancing and sports day races, and were happily dragged around the funfair stalls set up in the sports ground, guests and children all trying their luck at shooting down a row of ducks or hooping a toy elephant.

The weekend then kicked off with supper in the candlelit garden at Lakshmi House and finished with a Grand Finale supper on the beach under strings of fairy lights. It felt and looked magical.

The party was at my personal invitation and three suppers required a fair few bottles of wine. Wine is expensive in India but some seventy-five miles down the coast is Pondicherry, which retains some independent legislative rights as a former French colony, including tax. Wine was much cheaper there. There are no demarcation lines as such between Pondi and Tamil Nadu, but customs officers do lurk and it was too much of a risk to cross the border in a car loaded with 200 bottles. By sea was the answer, in true *Whisky Galore!* style. Some Kovalam fishermen offered to pick up the contraband on Pondi's beach in the dead of night. JR sat there surrounded by wine boxes, waiting for the boats to arrive from Kovalam, a distance of sixty-five miles, getting more nervous by the minute. I was trying to get an update from him on the phone from the UK, but he became incoherent as time went by. He obviously needed some Dutch courage and luckily was surrounded by it! Finally, the boats arrived and safely delivered the booty to Kovalam. India's very acceptable red and white Sula wine was enjoyed over a candlelit supper in the garden of Lakshmi House and at the Grand Finale supper on the beach illuminated with strings of fairy lights.

As fireworks rose from a fishing boat on the sea at the Grand Finale beach party, filling the night sky for all the village to enjoy, I became reflective about my eighty years and how I traded a leisurely retirement for one so unexpected and rewarding. I thought back to those early days at PUPS and its major makeover which successfully turned it into a happy and productive school. New classrooms and a dining hall were built there and another nine of various shapes, sizes, uses and locations have gone up over the years under the leadership of our now master builders, JR and Ali.

The opening of the High School (now Higher Secondary School) was a never-to-be-forgotten highlight and the excitement I felt when the first 240 students lined up for Assembly with the headmaster and teachers, raised the Indian flag and sang their National Anthem. A goose bumps moment. There are now a thousand pupils.

I had happily watched the school building go up, and when it was just bricks and mortar I longed for it to be filled with the sound of happy and stimulated students. I wanted it to buzz. And buzz it has. The students and teachers have created an incredible atmosphere of energy and their sheer joy of learning and teaching is very evident. Little wonder that it attracts the best headmaster and teachers as its reputation grows for its academic and sporting results as well as pastoral care.

While the fireworks continued to entertain my guests and the village, my thoughts turned to the sponsored children, thousands of them since the scheme was set up in 2005. They make me so happy because they all come from deprived homes, many of them living in very difficult circumstances but, like Venkat, they all grasp the opportunities given to them. They emerge victorious from the care of the Venkat Trust with qualifications paving the way for a bright and fulfilling future. They are delightful and confident and as they climb the ladder of their chosen careers, they know that for them, their families and their future families, poverty is a thing of the past.

★★★

The journey has continued and five years on I'm still at the helm, happy in the knowledge that the future is assured under the dedicated care of our younger trustees.

Writing this book with Lindsay and looking back over my four score years and five has been an extraordinary experience. There have been good times and bad times but many more good ones. I loved my globe-trotting days and many experiences I've shared with Lindsay running the Empire and building a charity in an Indian fishing village.

My very special friendship with JR and the joy we've had in seeing the Venkat Trust grow and prosper have been wonderful; I have enormous admiration for him. He agreed to take on the Kovalam end of the Trust in memory of his brother when he was a gauche 29-year-old and has triumphed every inch of the way.

Ours is a success story, or as JR would say in his delightful English, 'We've done a little OK'.

This extraordinary journey would never have happened had I not met the boy on the beach.

Dear Venkat, you did not die in vain.

EPILOGUE
SLIDING DOORS

Success comes at a cost and with more and more children thriving at our schools, most seize the opportunity to go on to university or vocational training. The bill for fees increases every year but the rewards are great – further education brings qualifications, which in turn promise fulfilling careers and the end of poverty.

Sylvia's early decision that every single penny raised would go to Kovalam and that all expenses in this country would be paid by the UK trustees, including their own air fares to India, has proved a winner. People love to know that their donations are going to improving education in the village, rather than the charity's salaries and costs in the UK. There can't be many whose 'paid out' column in their bank statements is a blank.

If the material in this book has affected you, and you would like to know more about the Venkat Trust, or to donate to our work, please visit www.venkattrust.org.uk.

We are eternally grateful for any help you can give. Everything that spreads awareness about the Venkat Trust is genuinely changing lives and providing real futures for some of the brightest young people we've ever encountered.

The authors will be donating their royalties to the Venkat Trust.

Thank you.

Sylvia Holder and Lindsay Swan

ACKNOWLEDGEMENTS

Our thanks to everyone who has helped *Accidental Lives* on its way to publication. The spark of the idea for the book came to us as we were relaxing on a rice boat on the Kerala Backwaters. Families and friends have encouraged us along the way and ploughed through our various drafts of the book.

Margaret Drabble has been our fellow traveller to Zambia and Kovalam, as has Piers Brendon, both always the very best of company. Brian Jackman's encyclopaedic knowledge of all things African hugely enriched our adventures in Zambia. Naren Chetty has become one of the Venkat Trust's staunchest supporters, a frequent visitor to Kovalam and shares Sylvia's passion for cricket. We thank them all for their kind words.

We are grateful to Bryony Sutherland, whose masterful edit gave us the confidence to believe our book could be published.

Thanks too to our publisher, Black Spring Press Group, for guiding our book to publication.

We gratefully acknowledge the many people who have brought joy to our lives over the years and provided material for our story.

We thank the Venkat Trust's trustees Nick Goslett, Sarah da Silva, John Whelan, Natalie Lee and Frankie Knight and our volunteers Emma Holder, Alex Smallman, Sandra Huggett and Expat Academy, who give so generously of their time and skills. And of course, our wonderful supporters.

Sylvia acknowledges and thanks her family and friends for their love and encouragement, particularly brother John, niece Emma and friend Sarah.

Lindsay acknowledges with love and thanks Richard, Ben, Georgina, Kirsty and Andy and her grandchildren Orla and Joe. Also, her sister Angela and friend Mary.

Finally, we thank the people of Kovalam, most notably the incomparable JR, Ali and Aarthi, who have contributed so much to the success of the Venkat Trust. Their friendship brings us both the most enormous pleasure and fun.

And of course we remember Venkat, the boy on the beach, who is forever missed.